the Try Angle

A New *Slant* on Life!

STEPHANIE STAPLES

The Try Angle—A New Slant on Life
© MMXVIII, by Stephanie Staples

Disclaimer: The purpose of this book is to educate and entertain. It is a true story and the characters and events are real. In some cases, the names, descriptions and locations have been changed, condensed or combined for storytelling purposes but the overall chronology is an accurate depiction of the author's memory of the experience. Tips in this book are intended for general guidance only and are not specific to any individual reader. Readers are encouraged to seek professional advice and neither the author nor publisher shall be liable or responsible for any loss or damage arising, or alleged to arise from, (directly or indirectly) any information or suggestion in this book.

If you are interested in purchasing additional/or bulk copies of _The Try Angle_ please contact Stephanie Staples at 204.227.2165 or visit YourLifeUnlimited.ca.

Inspirational, psychology, motivation, self-help, personal growth

Published by Your Life, Unlimited

Illustrations by John B. Junson
Cover photo by Teri Hofford
Cover design by Kimb Williams

To all these professionals I also get to call friends, thank you for sharing your talents!

ISBN-13: 978-1981917563
ISBN-10:198191756X

Dedication

To Liliana Scarnati, my mom,
my greatest fan, my beacon.

All these crazy things I try, I dedicate
to this woman who lived her life
for others, selflessly gave decade
after decade and never could have
imagined living a life like the
one she gave me.

My pride is exceeded only by my love.

This one's for you Mom.

To you, the reader, the learner, the seeker,
the adventurer, the curious–thank you
for caring enough to try.

Contents

Part Three - The Next New Beginning

Squirrels

When you see this little cutie, you will find a random, sometimes related, sometimes unrelated thought that pops into my mind while writing that may or may not be of interest to you. But it's of interest to me so I'm writing it. So there. Gina, my youngest daughter (You'll hear more about this feisty little spitfire!) used to say, "Stop saying *squirrel*—no one knows what you are talking about!" I doth protest dearest daughter who knows just about everything. *Au contraire*, in fact almost everyone knows what I am talking about. But for the two percent of you who don't . . . YouTube "Carl & Ellie's Story", it may be the most poignant five minutes of your day and it is actually completely appropriate to view prior to reading this book. Go ahead–watch it now. I'll wait. Actually maybe I'll go watch it again.

Aw. I watched it again and I still love it. Did you?

Okay, now enjoy *The Try Angle!*

Part One

the new beginning

Chapter One

the try angle–start here

To try — to attempt an activity with the
understanding that it may not be successful.

HAVE YOU ever sung in public, taken a drum lesson or done Parkour? Well, neither had I.

According to my mom (and my birth certificate), I was born on November 13, 1965, which means a couple of things.

First, I turned 50 on Friday the 13th, 2015. How ominous to have such a big birthday on this inauspicious day. I wonder if there is a deep meaning there? Nah, probably not.

Second, if Statistics Canada is correct, for a female born in 1965, if I'm lucky I have about twenty-four years left. Yikes–that doesn't seem like enough. How many do you have left?

I had been pondering how to roll into my next couple of decades and I'd finally decided that I would step-up the famed Bucket List with a very personalized 50/50 List. Have you heard of it? Probably not because, well, I invented it and it got me jazzed!

A Bucket List is comprised of things you want to do before you die. My list would encompass things I committed to doing in my fiftieth year. Fifty 'Try's" in my 50th year. The immediacy of this 50/50 List made it super appealing to me because there was no time to talk myself out of these challenges!

It seems that birthdays that end with a zero can be especially taxing for some strange reason, and when one particular birthday starts with a five and ends with and zero, it's enough to put some people into a mild state of depression.

But I am one of the lucky ones. Oh sure, I have age related stuff–osteoarthritis, degenerative disk disease, strange dots appearing in random places on my body and the odd stray hair popping out in the wrong place (Where did those tweezers go?) but overall I am strong, fit and healthy.

Of course, more not-so-subtle signs of aging are going on too. Like when did they start making the writing on bottle so small, memory issues and–um–I forgot the other things. But still I am smart, capable and independent. What else can a girl, er, older woman, ask for?

Challenges! I wanted challenges. I wanted to be pushed, pulled and dragged into the next half century and this was the year to do it!

I wanted an eclectic mix of experiences that would inspire me physically, emotionally, socially, professionally, intellectually, spiritually–every which way. Sure, even sexually–why not?

Years ago, when I was explaining the birds and the bees to my youngest daughter, in her disgust she said, "You and Dad didn't do that, did you?" To which I replied the only answer that seemed appropriate at the time, "Just three times, to get you three kids. And it was worth it, just so you know." How was I to know that she would be telling her friends at school our little family secret and how distraught she would be when her friends finally convinced her that she had been duped. Don't kids have anything better to talk about than their parents' sex life–or lack thereof?

Anyway I digress, back to my challenges. I wanted them to run the gamut. I imagined that some things would cost money and some would be free. There would be big things, small things, solo things and things that would involve others. Private and public things, philanthropic and selfish things, local and global things. Any things!

I didn't know what would be on the list, but what I did know was that I could not create it alone. Even though I have a sizable comfort zone, I knew that if I was responsible for writing the list, the items would fall within the limits of my zone and I didn't want that. I wanted to grow. So I asked for suggestions from people in different walks of life, from different professions, and with different passions and ethnicities. I asked people who knew me and even complete strangers. No holds barred, no limits—anything could go on the list. However, I reserved the right to negotiate, debate and adjust the suggestions. That only seemed fair.

Even before the project officially started, just the act of creating the list, gathering those suggestions and seeing people start to do their own version of the 50/50 List was already a win for me. Sometimes people just need to hear about another person's experience to spark an idea of their own and then they are off to the races.

What would you put on your list? Here are some questions to help you build it:

- What would make you brave the unknown?
- What would make you feel proud of yourself and/or help you better understand people who are different from you?
- What could add a little more fun and excitement to your life and give you something to look forward to?
- What have you been curious about?
- What will give you something to talk about when someone says, "What's new?"
- What might surprise you, scare you, fulfil you?
- What might help you bond with people you love, create an experience you might have missed out on or learn something new?

THOSE THINGS and more are what my 50/50 List was about. You don't have to be turning 50 to create one. You just have to be purposeful, deliberate and intentional about making those experiences come to life.

I wasn't dreading turning 50 at all. In reality I was celebrating the fact that I *got* to turn 50 when so many people don't get that chance.

When the journey began I had no idea that the 50/50 List would lead me through one the best years of my life to date. My theme was *Grow* and that's exactly what I did. Whatever age you are I hope *The Try Angle* inspires you to have a new slant on life.

Okay—ready? Let's grow!

Chapter Two

get out of your own way

WHEN I PUBLISHED *When Enlightening Strikes–Creating a Mindset for Uncommon Success* it was a labour of love. I had that book in my head for five years and I just couldn't get it out. It went through three reincarnations before the final book was released.

The first version was a very didactic, "coachy", do this, do that, type of book. Yuck. The second was therapy (for me), an upchuck of past unpleasant baggage that I apparently had to get out of my system. Double yuck.

The third was the book you can hold in your hand, one that I am proud of, the one that should have you laughing, crying and learning almost simultaneously. It's the one I was scared to release lest people think poorly of the person who wrote the book with a first section entitled *Confessions of a Motivational Speaker*. With the release of this book came the first realization that we don't have to know *how* everything will turn out.

We must get our big fat heads around the crazy idea that we have to please everyone, that everyone has to like us or agree with us. That we are not good enough, fast enough, or strong enough. That people will judge us, look at us, laugh at us, and talk about us.

I hate to be the bearer of bad news but the truth is that not everyone will think you are great or nice or awesome or the best cook, parent, or volleyball player on the planet. Some people will think the decisions you make are stupid or silly, and the goals you set are too big, too small, too unattainable, will take too much out of you, are impossible, a waste of time, annoying, bad, selfish–fill in your own adjective here.

Shocker… sometimes you will be wrong. The good news is that mostly it's not life-threatening. I may not know you personally but I'm guessing it's likely you've been wrong a time or two in your life (maybe even recently–gasp!) and you survived.

No matter how much you give, share, have, do, contribute or accomplish, it will not be enough for some people. Get over it. It simply won't be enough. To live your life unlimited, as I assume you want to do, you need to be okay with that. Awaiting perfection is a long and winding road to nowhere. Thank you to The Beatles for that analogy.

If we look at all the reasons not to start something we will have no shortage of them: commitments, responsibilities, alternate priorities. You may have noticed that the first letter of those excuses spells CRAP. Now while those may all be very good reasons, if we look at them as reasons we will be stuck, blocked, and/or trapped. We will go nowhere anytime soon–kind of like trying to get to town on a stationary bicycle. If we look at them as excuses though, as the smart people we are, we can find a way over, under, through and around them! Yes, we can.

I'm not sure if anyone has told you before but the "right" time might never come. In fact, it's very likely you will die waiting for the right time, a better time or the "perfect" time. I get that there may be a lot of CRAP going on in your life right now. I get that you believe that as soon as you have a handle on it, you're sure you will move in the direction you want to go, but I beg to differ. In fact, I have bad news. Just when you wade through the current CRAP in your life, ready or not… you got it–more CRAP! This time it may be different or unexpected CRAP but as long as you are breathing, there will always be CRAP in your life. Yep. Sorry.

It is important to note that this is not the same as your life always being crappy. Your life can be fab despite or even *because* of the CRAP going on.

You think you don't have enough time, money, energy, motivation, or resources. Define enough please?

Fact–you don't need enough, there may never be enough, and as soon as people get enough they typically want more enough, whatever the heck enough is. *Enough!* Start where you are, with what you have. You just need some. *Some* is good enough. Period.

Getting out of your own way will untether, unanchor and unchain you from a life of mediocrity, boredom and conventionality. If you want that type of life that's fine–there is nothing wrong with that; but then why are you still reading? Getting out of your own way will allow you to see things from a new and fresh perspective and to problem-solve in ways that will make your life (and likely the lives of others) easier.

Getting out of your own way will impact people in different ways. It will inspire people in your life–your kids, your family, your colleagues and even complete strangers. However, I feel the need to prepare you–it will completely annoy the heck out of other people. It will make some people run the other way when they see you coming. They might even… oh no… unfriend you! Trust me… don't you hate when people say that, "Trrrrrrussssst me."? (Cue the hissing, slithery snake) But seriously, trust me, the benefits of who you will meet and what you will experience will far outweigh the losses.

Getting out of your own way will allow you to "grow on the inside" as I used to tell my kids when they had to do something they didn't want to do. When you grow on the inside you can become more open-minded, less judgemental, smarter, more savvy, more worldly, less needy, more intriguing, even more attractive because people are drawn to interesting people. Admit it–even you *are*, right? I mean, who would you rather spend an hour talking to–the trophy polisher or the trophy winner?

You cannot move forward without getting out of your own way. No one else is stopping you. No one else is blocking you. No circumstance, no people, no situation. *You* are stopping you. Of course, what do I know? I could be wrong, but I've already been wrong once, maybe twice in my life, so I don't think so.

Many people poo-poo "motivational speakers" and "self-help books" and that's okay. I have a huge problem with a lot of the rah, rah stuff myself. I just don't buy it, but shhhh, I still have to make a living you know. ;)

Here are some examples of motivational mantras with which I disagree:

> You can have it all. *No, you can't actually, everything comes at a cost.*
>
> You can be/have/do anything you want. *False. I'm 5'2". I'm not going to be a basketball star.*
>
> Never give up. *Are you crazy? Of course you have to give up sometimes or you might die trying, you might lose something more precious or a hundred other reasons why giving up is sometimes a great choice.*
>
> Try it, you'll like it. *Maybe you will but there is an equally good chance you won't.*

Of course, as I've mentioned previously, I could be wrong. What do I know? Then again, I'm a mom, so in all likelihood I'm right.

A few years back I went to see a physiotherapist for a problem with my right hand. Upon assessment she asked me the question that healthcare providers love to ask, "On a scale of one to ten, how is your pain?" I was a little embarrassed to tell her that my pain was only a two, but I just knew that something wasn't right with my hand. To my relief, she did not make me feel like a grown-up sissy; she was, in fact, very pleased.

And then she said words that changed everything for me. "Most people wait until their pain level is much higher. When you come in with your pain at a two, it's harder to diagnosis but it's much easier to treat. When people come in with their pain at an eight, it's much easier to diagnosis but it's much harder to treat."

Now you may think this is a squirrel moment but stay with me. What she said isn't just about physio treatments, it's about life. Generally this is how we live it. We ignore problems, issues and challenges when they are a two. We think that if we ignore them they will go away, but often they escalate and suddenly we are faced with an eight and it's a big deal to "treat".

We are bored with life at a level two but we ignore the nudges, the feelings, the intuition. Then "suddenly" we feel miserable, stuck, blocked and trapped. We start treating the people we love the most, who matter to us most and who care about us most, terribly. Not because they did something wrong, but because we are unhappy. We forget what we liked, we forget what jazzed us up, we forget who we were and we stop thinking about who we want to be.

In Neil Donald Walsch's book, *Conversations with God*, he talks about the "Have, Do, Be" philosophy that many people tend to live by. He suggests most people think this way, "If I *have* this thing called money, I will *do* the things that people with money do and then I will *be* happy." He suggests flipping it to, "If I *do* things that happy people do, I will *have* the things that happy people have and then I will *be* happy!"

Be this thing called happy. Stop waiting for a better time or circumstance. The world needs you to be your best–to shine, to share, to discover, to be a catalyst for positive change. If you forget what you loved it's time to rediscover it. If you are due for some new adventures, experiences and relationships now is the perfect time.

I'm excited for you because I have seen the show. I know how it ends once you go beyond thinking and start implementing! That's when life starts getting exciting! Every day you are writing the story of your life. Write an exciting script. Write a story that people want to hear about.

You have been writing your story for a long time. You may have looked at it from this angle and that angle but you probably have never looked at it from *The Try Angle*.

Chapter Three

something about mary

I MET MARY at an event called Mindcamp. A creativity conference for people from all walks of life and a plethora of professions, Mindcamp is held annually near Toronto, Canada. The setting is not your typical conference hotel; it is a YMCA camp in beautiful Lake Geneva, Ontario (and I highly recommend it or any other creativity conference).

What I love about the Mindcamp experience is it draws an eclectic blend of people rather than delegates who are all in the same profession. Mindcamp is all the things you enjoy most about a conference without all the stuffy, pretentious attitudes that benefit no one.

At this conference there were people from Disney and people from sexual health. There were dog trainers, lawyers, graphic designers, entrepreneurs and yes, motivational speakers too! Everyone there, no matter what they did for a living, knew that they and their job would benefit from being more creative.

In that sea of people was one very special person whose name was Mary.

Mary, with her blue-tinged hair, stylish clothes and her long, purple fingernails, must have been in her mid-eighties. I did a double take when I saw her. I couldn't imagine what a woman of that age would be doing at a creativity conference–but my first thought was, "I want to be like her when I grow up! When I am in my golden years I want to want to come to a creativity conference. I want to desire surrounding myself with people who are different from me. I want to be curious, to be continually learning and growing and evolving and having new experiences." Heck, I want to do that now, never mind when I am eighty-something!

As luck would have it, Mary chose a seat beside me in the very next session. As we introduced ourselves she spread out her books and supplies on the table. I could hardly wait to ask her "my" question. It's the last question I ask every guest on my radio show. . . "If you could tell people only one thing, what would that one thing be?"

Mary didn't miss a beat; she didn't hesitate. Instead she confidently picked up a pen and pulled my notebook over to her side of the table. She looked me right in the eyes and I knew I was about to hear something very profound. I could feel my eyes open wider and I put my listening ears on.

"There is a very good chance you will live to be 100 years old," she said as she drew a big circle on my page and divided it into quarters. As she pointed to each section she explained, "The first quarter of your life your parents pretty much made every decision for you. The second quarter of your life pretty much every decision you made was for the benefit of or influenced by your family or partner. The last quarter of your life will likely find your children making decisions for you." "This quarter," she said as she tapped her pen down repeatedly on the third section, "this quarter is the only time in your life that you get to make decisions just for you."

Then she put the pen down, put her hands on my shoulders and stared me down. "Promise me that the decisions you make at this time of your life will be for you."

"I promise." I said, as I was making this sudden earth-shattering decision to a total stranger.

What she told me that day was an eye-opening game changer. I get to make decisions just for me. Hmmm. What a concept? What would that even be like? I could hardly imagine. As a woman, a caregiver, a wife, and a mom I was hard-wired to yield to others.

As a woman who was already most likely in her last quarter Mary definitely got my attention.

No matter what quarter of your life you are in, I believe Mary's advice is worth considering. Of course, you will still make decisions with others in mind. I'm not talking about living twenty-five years completely selfishly without considering anyone else. But what if some of the decisions you make (more than you used to for sure) can be about you? What if some of those decisions should be about you, need to be about you and have to be about you?

The Try Angle is about you. No one else but you. And when you benefit, grow, and evolve others will vicariously as well. Or they might not. That gets to be okay too.

Chapter Four

suspend and adjust judgement

THERE ARE certain characteristics about myself that I have been working on improving for a long time. Reducing judgement is close to the top of the list. I dislike when I judge others; it doesn't make me feel good about myself and it certainly doesn't help the other person.

I told myself that judging people does not make them so, that it only makes me judgemental… a quality I do not want to own. It wasn't until a conversation with a colleague, Jessica Pettitt, on this topic that I changed my view on the subject.

Jessica says, "We must judge to be able to show up safe and prepared. We write someone else's story based on our lived experiences. The key is that the story may not be 100% accurate. We need to leave room for edits and treat our story about them as a *draft*. This draft can be printed triple spaced with extra wide margins, and then with curiosity, generosity, vulnerability, and authenticity, we can connect with someone and seek their edits and update our draft with their truth."

This was such a great concept and a visual that I could wrap my head around. I wondered if I could apply it to myself as well. Could I apply it to my story? Who I am, who I am supposed to be? What can I or can't I do? What should I or should I not do? What do other people expect of me, from me, for me?

Am I letting judgements that have been placed upon me by

myself or by others based on old or limiting beliefs, presumptions, past experiences, etc., stop me from progressing?

One of my favourite techniques is to ask not if I can use information but how can I use information I glean. How many different ways, in what areas of my personal and/or professional life, can I combine it with another idea, etc.? Doing this has added value to my life in too many ways to describe. Try it! Don't ask if, ask how.

I don't know everything, but what I know for sure is that if I am casting judgement on others, so it is that they are probably casting judgement on me.

So many of us spend far too much time worrying about those who don't even know us, care about us, love us or even think about us. We expend time, effort, money, and resources trying to please these people. We let these people stop us from trying the very things that might help us be better human beings.

Sometimes it's our judgement about the judgement that may be preventing us from trying, and therefore, growing. And sometimes, if we are really, really honest, we might even be using these people as excuses to not try. "Well, I would but… " Speaking of buts, not butts, but buts, there is no room for buts in *The Try Angle*. Buts are Try-Killers.

To utilize *The Try Angle*, you need to learn to suspend and adjust self-judgement and to realize that what other people think of you is actually none of your concern. What other people think of you is often more of a reflection of where they are at than where you are at. It's not easy for the people pleasers among us, but it's the only way.

Chapter Five

encourage curiosity

The foundation for *The Try Angle* is curiosity. If you aren't curious– about outcomes, answers, possibilities, the world and yourself in particular, then either I have to try to inspire you to get curious or we are sort of done already. Curiosity is key. You were born with it; it's in there somewhere. For some it's probably just buried a little deeper than for others.

If you like the technical stuff, perhaps it might interest you to know about a couple of different types of curiosity. Epistemic curiosity is driven by the desire for knowledge, whereas diversive curiosity is motivated by feelings of boredom. Personally, I don't care what the driver is–I just want you to get curious again, like you were when you were a child.

Imagine yourself asking interesting questions, talking to new people, wondering, digging deeper, asking why and how come more than you have in years.

What if, "What if… " became your mantra? What if… followed by positive answers first!

Put "What if… " up on your wall, write it on your bathroom mirror (with a dry erase marker), put an electronic sticky on your computer screen, tattoo it on the inside of your eyelids! Make a list of a hundred "What ifs"–the crazier the better. They don't have to be doable, they don't have to be realistic, they don't have to be date sensitive. The whole purpose is to open up dialogue between you and yourself, and maybe later you will add in a partner, child, friend, spouse, parent, stranger or group to the equation. Take twenty minutes out of your life and do this. I know you think you can't, but you can. You will find some things of particular interest once you get past about fifty-two!

Limitless possibilities and an unending stream of conversations in your mind will ensue, each one connecting like a mind map to something else, spurring on ideas and generating energy and excitement as it goes.

Sometimes the dialogue leads to, "No way." Sometimes it's, "Not yet." Sometimes it's, "Maybe." But once in a while it's an absolute, "Yes!" No matter the result of the conversation, just doing the exercise causes the trap door on our minds to open just a tiny bit more and let a little light in.

Encouraging curiosity is what it's all about! What do you do to encourage curiosity? What can you do to encourage curiosity? And most importantly, what will you do to encourage curiosity?

Chapter Six

kaizen your way to success

KAIZEN is my secret sauce. *Kaizen* is the reason for my "success." *Kaizen* is how I try to live my life day in and day out and I hope you can recognize the power in this two-syllable Japanese word.

Kaizen means small, continuous improvement. Everyone can benefit from sprinkling a little bit of Kaizen in their life and, for all you Type A perfectionists out there, this word can be the ultimate game changer.

Imagine a zero to ten scale. Most of us love to do things we are good at, the things that come easily and effortlessly to us. We like to do things around the eight, nine, ten level, right? If we know that we can't perform at eight, nine, or ten, we often take a pass—which means we are at zero. Are you with me here?

Kaizen asks, "What is the smallest thing I can do regularly to lean me in the direction that I want to go?" Kaizen asks. "On that zero to ten scale, what would a four look like?" Gasp–a four, I know what you're thinking–you can't possibly perform at a measly four. That would not be acceptable. Maybe. And maybe not.

Some of the most recent research suggests that setting a goal that increases your capacity by four to eleven percent may just be the sweet spot. Lower than four percent you don't get the benefit of momentum, and at higher than eleven percent you may find yourself overwhelmed and not continue.

You might not think "four" matters but if you could improve

your relationship by four to eleven percent would that be significant enough to count? If you could get in four to eleven percent better shape, would that matter? I'm guessing it would!

Four, five and six matter!

You can't do everything but you can do some things. You can't help everybody but you can help somebody. You can't have it all, but you deserve to have more... (fun, adventure, learnings, creativity, stimulation, laughter or fill in your word here). You deserve more and you can have more in whatever situation you find yourself. Your circumstance doesn't necessarily have to change but your mindset may have to. Do you have any idea what an unexpected gift that may be? Once your mindset changes, your circumstances may just change as well!

Ignite your curiosity, apply a Kaizen mindset and complete *The Try Angle*.

Chapter Seven

honour your commitment

I'M NOT TALKING ABOUT pledging your undying love forever. I'm not talking about inking it into your skin for a lifetime. I'm talking about making a commitment to yourself, one that you'd take as seriously as one you made to your child or a to your parent on their deathbed. A commitment to try. You don't have to love the things you try. You don't have to be perfect, or even good at them, you just have to commit to giving them a whirl.

With the commitment (and you may have to do it a few times before you believe me) will come the belief that very often it is not even about the actual "activity" that you are attempting but more about what you will learn and experience along the way. Perhaps it is the person you will learn from and/or the opportunity for them to teach; perhaps it's in a relationship you will form along the way. Maybe it's about what happens in the preliminary planning or in the post event debrief. It might be about who else is inspired along the way. Or it might be something you never even find out about, but the ripple rolls on.

The commitment says you are worth it, you do what you say you are going to do, you are dependable, reliable. It says that despite the highly likely chance that you perceive a lack of time, money, energy, support or motivation, *you* are resourceful, *you* are dedicated to results, *you* are action-oriented. *You do what you say you are going to do.* No matter how small the commitment, you honour it. You know it's not the size of the commitment that matters, it's doing it. *You are committed* to learning and growth.

Isn't this who you want to be?

Encourage curiosity, adopt a Kaisen mindset and honour your commitment. *That's The Try Angle.*

Part Two

try, try
and try again

Try 1

stand by me

I SPEAK for a living so I'm no stranger to a microphone or audiences or "performing".

I like music and, in fact, I like singing. I sing in the shower, I sing in the car and I sing in the kitchen. I don't know why people always leave the room or turn up the radio when I sing; I try not to take it personally. I can sing. Maybe not well, but I can sing–heck, everyone can sing!

But apparently just because you *can* do something doesn't mean you *should*.

It is the first day of my 50/50 challenge, my birthday, my fiftieth birthday. The Hub and I had planned a lovely birthday party and during the party, unbeknownst to the guests, after twenty-seven years of marriage we will be renewing our wedding vows. The only one in on the surprise is Gina who will be performing the *I Do, Take Two* ceremony.

What better time to meet my first challenge, to sing in public. This Try was given to me by my "sister from a different mister", Lea Brovedani. I had a visceral reaction when she suggested this to me. I literally had a stomach ache just *thinking* about doing this, but what better an audience than the fifty people who I've personally hand-picked to come to my party. They already love me, it's not like they are going to walk out, or worse yet, laugh. Are they??

But how to pull this off? Hmmm.

I call my musician friend, Gentil Mis, who will be singing for the event (also a surprise for my husband Randy–who will be known henceforth as The Hub–and the guests) and tell him about my idea, half hoping he will talk me out of it so I can at least say, "I tried!"

But no. He thinks its a stellar idea and invites me to his studio to practice with his band the night before the event. The night before!! Ugh!

Google my buddy Gentil–we think he's fab! Our favourite song 2+9 inspired The Hub to engrave my new wedding ring with 2+9. Sweet!

Because it was sung at our first wedding, I choose the song "Stand By Me." Isn't that sweet? Mostly I choose it because it's very short and the range of notes isn't too crazy.

As the time to practice gets closer, my feet get colder and colder. My stomach is churning by the time I arrive at the studio. This is a terrible idea. It's one thing embarrassing yourself in front of strangers, but in front of close friends and family–that's even worse.

As a professional speaker I should have known better. Having a crowd of 1000 strangers is far less pressure than having a crowd of 100 with one person you love in it.

I'm having second, third, fourth and fifth thoughts about this idea. I am cursing no one in particular and me in general. Someone should stop me when I get these ideas!

That evening I practice with the band–a whole, real band! I gotta say, with music and a "back up" singer, it is actually a strange kind of fun, mostly because there is no audience. They give me tips like which words to punch up and how to hold the mic for the most impact. Mostly they didn't laugh or have any visible looks of distaste on their faces.

After an hour they say, "We are ready." I think, "Maybe you guys are ready, but I'm nowhere near ready. I can't even get my lips around the word ready." "What if I make a mistake?" I ask, probably more than once. "Just keep going, just keep going," they say.

They encourage me and make me feel like I might actually be able to pull this off and then they send me on my way.

While I can't say I feel pretty good, I can at least say I feel better than when I went into the studio. "Maybe I can pull this off?"

I love the word "studio". I have started calling my office a studio and I feel more creative already!

I practice my song all the way home. "I got this!" I tell myself over and over.

People arrive for my birthday party and eat and drink and visit as party-goers do. After an hour or so we ask them to sit down and we direct their attention to a video, which they have no choice but to watch. While the guests are distracted watching the video of our life together (insert possible yawn here), The Hub and I leave to change our clothes and assume our positions.

When the video is over the lights come on and it's "showtime." I am petrified–not about renewing my vows, about singing. The stuff my stomach do not know what to do–come up, go down or both.

I stand at the end of the makeshift "aisle", the music starts and everyone stares at me, most likely wondering why this birthday party suddenly looks like a wedding, and why I am standing at the end of the aisle with a microphone. No one knows, not even The Hub (especially not The Hub) what is about to happen.

"I don't got this after all!" I think to myself. "I've changed my mind. How do I get out of this?" I feel my heart palpitating. I'm certain people can see it pulsing from under my dress. "Gawd, I hope the other 49 challenges aren't this awful."

Then I think of *The Try Angle*. Ignite Curiosity–What if I sing in public? Adopt a Kaizen Mindset–Not weekly, just do it once, and you never have to do this again. Honour Your Commitment–This is it!

I plant my feet. I breathe. I look straight ahead, eyes only on my man. I lift the microphone high to my mouth–differently from the way I hold it when I speak. I hold it the way they told me to–like a diva!

I hear an audible gasp from the crowd. They don't say it but I know they are thinking, "Oh my God, she's going to sing! She can't sing. Can she sing? Oh my God, she's going to sing!"

The intro music starts and there is no going back. *"When the night has come and the land is dark..."* I give it my best. This short song has only two verses that I practiced a lot. Still in my over-anxious state, I stumble over the lyrics in the second verse. I hear the band's words in my ear... "Just keep going, just keep going."

I sing myself up the aisle and The Hub is smiling the biggest smile and mouthing the chorus, "Stand By Me." When I get to him, I put the microphone to his lips and his unsteady voice singing into the microphone is literally music to my ears. We finish the song together in our imperfection.

It's a fitting testament to our twenty-seven years of beautiful imperfection where we just kept going, through thick and thin, we just kept going.

And so the first challenge was complete, done, checked off! A corny but sweet move that stretched me in a way I would never had attempted without being challenged.

It flattered my man. It taught me the benefits of learning from pros, having backups in your corner, and assuming people are there to support not judge.

In the end, even when you think you are going to die, you usually aren't.

Try 2

go within

MEDITATION. I've heard it's supposed to be awesome! I read that twenty minutes of meditating is equivalent of two hours of sleep. I read that it is good for the body, mind and soul. There must be something to this practice and I want to find out what it is. Nobody ever complains that they are too relaxed, too calm or that they are over-meditated. ;)

But I'm an extrovert. I like to talk and I get my energy from people. The thought of being quiet, still, silent, and alone on purpose had little to no appeal for me. In fact, it frightened me some.

I do some research and find online courses, in-person courses and meditation Apps. I research this type of meditation and that type of meditation. Who knew there were so many different kinds?

I decide that an in-person session is likely the best route for me and I talk a friend into accompanying me to a class. She is a good sport as we sit in the dark, cross-legged on the floor and we chant "Ommm... " like we are supposed to. My mind thinks, "If someone walks into the room right now and finds out we paid good money to sit on the floor and do nothing they will think we are a little unstable."

It feels like everyone else in the class knows what to do, but my mind does not know how to be quiet (yet, I add optimistically).

The instructor says, "Put the

Yet is my new favourite word. It acknowledges that I do not yet possess the skill but implies optimism that I will! Like, "I'm not good at math, yet!"

Omm in your heart," but I hear, "Put the pom in your cart." Now all I can think about is my shopping list. "I need toilet paper, bananas, what else?... ummm, a pomegranate would be nice."

Oh, I mean... "Ommmm." "Right, we are meditating," I remind myself.

"And, oh yeah, I need razors which reminds me I'd better shave my legs soon, which makes me think about what I'm going to wear to the event on the weekend, does anything need to be dry cleaned and while I am at the dry cleaners... ummm... "

Oh, I mean... "Ommmm." "Man, I really suck at this!"

I finally realize that this is not the direction my mind is supposed to be going and, for some reason, this strikes me funny. I start to giggle to myself. I am trying to keep the giggle tucked in, but you know how the more you try to tuck it in, the more it wants to bubble out? Well, that's what is happening. Soon my shoulders start to jiggle and then the giggle squeaks out of my lips. I'm jiggling and giggling and my friend opens her eyes and looks over at me... and you know how sometimes those giggles are a bit contagious? Well, that's what happens. I can't stop giggling and jiggling and then she starts as well and both of us are trying to stuff it down and be unnoticed but it doesn't work. Eventually we are asked to leave the room. Our "Ommm" turned into an "Oops".

Kicked out of mediation class, epic fail!

Clearly this challenge has not been met. Yet. I have ignited the curiosity, I am committed to trying. I think I just need to Kaizen this a little bit more. Maybe an hour is a bit much to ask from a beginner. Maybe I should just start with a couple of minutes.

So that's what I do. I research some other types of meditation and commit to practicing at home until I get better at it.

There is this one type of meditation where you stare into a mirror–like super close until your face gets all distorted. It sounds like an awful idea to stare at my face for an uncomfortable amount of time but I decide to do it anyway.

I lie down on my bedroom floor in front of the full-length

mirrored closet door, just a few inches away from it as they recommend. Ick, it feels terribly uncomfortable staring at yourself like that. What I notice is that once I focus on my face it doesn't take long before my eyes begin to see fuzzy and the image gets distorted. It's super weird.

I try the candle meditation–I like that one. You stare at the flickering flame of a candle.

I try the 21 day *Meditation Challenge* from Oprah and Deepak Chopra and I really like that one; it's guided and that helps me a lot. I find myself looking forward to it each evening.

I try the slow walking meditation–which is painfully pokey. I try the labyrinth (which makes me a bit dizzy). I learn that there are both active and passive types of meditation.

I download *Insight Timer* which has thousands of meditations of every type and I really like the variety this provides. Some are music while others are guided. Some are both.

The Hub decides to come on board and we both start doing the ten-day, ten-minute *Headspace App*. He becomes hooked on this and incorporates it into his morning routine each day. He says he feels different. In fact, he is so calm that even his work buddies notice a difference. Cool!

I see a Meetup for Osho meditation. I have no idea what this is but The Hub and I decide to give it a go. Oh my, my oh my–it is active meditation to say the least. Now apparently there are 125 types of Osho meditation and the one we experience is... an experience to say the least.

For ten minutes we are standing up and we breathe fast out of our noses. We use our whole bodies to expel air (and some nasties) out of our noses. Note to Self: bring tissues! For the next ten minutes we get angry. Very, very angry. Pillow punching, fist banging, yelling, screaming, crying, stomping angry. Yes, I'm serious.

Then, once we've let the anger out, we say, "Who" and jump up and down slamming our heels into the ground and pushing our arms up into the air. This is supposed to impact our chakras. I don't

Sure wish I had worn the right bra for this, I had no idea we would be working out.

know anything about chakras (yet), but I know this is getting more peculiar by the minute.

Then we freeze in whatever position we are in and stay completely still for another ten minutes. If things hurt, too bad. If we are itchy, oh well. You get the idea, breathe through it.

Then we lie down and let everything that just happened assimilate for another ten minutes.

Oh, I forgot to mention–we do all this surrounded by strangers and… wait for it… blindfolded!

Uh-huh.

You can imagine our trepidation as we listened to the instructor explain what was about to happen in the next hour when all we thought we were going to do was sit in silence.

We did it and it was an interesting experience. A very interesting experience. I may try one of the other 124 Osho meditations next year, but for now I think I will stick with my App.

What I learned from this challenge is that there's not just one right way to do something, there are many right ways and sometimes you just have to keep trying until you find the right way for you.

Try 3

grit, grime and guts

My BB (Best Buddy) Marie and I have a history of pushing ourselves physically. I don't think that in the twenty odd years we've been friends we have ever "gone out for coffee"–we just always do things together. We bike, we run, we swim, we play Frisbee. We just like to move.

Most years Marie and I set out on a new physical challenge. We've done a half marathon (my favourite part was when she said, "I'm not talking anymore, you can talk if you want to, but I'm done." We did the Grouse Grind–a 2.9 kilometre climb up the face of Grouse Mountain (known as Mother Nature's StairMaster). We did a Try-A-Tri. (You'll have to read *When Enlightening Strikes* to read about that crazy experience). This year, to commemorate our 50th birthdays, we set out to do our first Gran Fondo–if you are not in the know yet, a Gran Fondo is not a person, it's "a long-distance road cycling event in which a large number of cyclists ride a marked route". This particular one was in the beautiful Qu'Appelle Valley region of Saskatchewan and was called The Spoke'n Hot (which we modestly thought was an

One of my other friends said to me, "Can't we just sit down for once? Do we always have to be moving?" And another said to her daughter about me, "Oh Steph is not the kind of friend you have coffee with, she is the kind of friend you do something with." Not sure if I've been insulted, but probably. Maybe I should work on "having coffee"?

appropriate title for us). They have a variety of distances to accommodate the various levels of riders, but we like to challenge ourselves, so together we decide to sign up for the 100 kilometre ride, which sounds challenging but doable. Unbeknownst to me, when Marie signs us up she decides we should do the 100 *mile* distance. (Yes, on purpose!) *No buena amiga!*

Marie and I are used to being slow in the events we enter. We are there for fun, exercise, and the experience. We are used to being clothed differently than the other "athletes" and having them look at us like we don't really belong. We are okay with all that. This "race" takes it to a whole new level though. We know it right from the start when we are the only ones going this distance without a road bike or clip-in cycling shoes. Uh-oh.

Nonetheless, we begin at 8 a.m. It's already 27°C and hot. We pedal our little hearts out; everyone passes us quite quickly but we are used to that. When we stop at the rest areas we notice that they have very little food, just snacks like bananas and candy. It's noon now and we are getting hungry for lunch. "Where's the lunch? They said there would be lunch?" We keep going until the rest stops are closing up. "Boo." We start to worry when no one has passed us for a long, long, long time. It's a circular route—we should be seeing other riders. We are tired and hungry, but we busy ourselves singing and amusing as BB's do. We pull over to take a break and that's when Marie's hubby calls to tell us that they called him looking for us (We had left his name as our emergency contact—was this an emergency?) "Looking for us? We are following the route so why are they looking for us?" Apparently we are MIA. Uh-oh again. We keep pedaling. And pedaling. And pedaling. Until we see a van, the race director's van.

We have been riding in the heat for nine hours, with little food (lunch had been served hours ago at the finish line) and not enough water. The race director tells us we are entering the length of time that endurance athletes ride, that it will be getting dark soon and it isn't safe to continue. Plus they are taking the course directions down. There is no choice; he pulls us from the course.

We want to continue! We want to finish. Tears leak out of my eyes. We aren't done nor are we spent, and we are definitely not finished! Devastatingly disappointed after working so hard for so long, with hurting hearts and no choice, we had to concede.

The consolation was not in the medal that they gave us anyway. It was in what the race director wrote to us afterwards… "You outperformed your equipment–248,900 people in the local area did not/would not attempt to do what you did. Celebrate the fact that you rode that distance in less than ideal circumstances, reflect on the lessons learned and plan for future success."

To try — to attempt an activity with the understanding that it may not be successful.

"I guess I am proud of our grit and for not giving up," I thought.

And then for a little icing on the cake, I read his final line, a tribute to the "motivational speaker" in me, "Gee, I sound like you!"

Try 4

yum?

I FIND MYSELF in a Scottish pub with some Scottish friends in Toronto. It's the first time for us and there are plenty of unusual items on the menu; it seems a perfect place to try my next Try–new foods.

I have heard of haggis before and certainly don't recall favourable reports. I ask my chum Helen what it is and she tells me, with a straight face, that it's a bird that runs around on a hill so it has one leg longer than the other.

Everyone's a comedian. I suspect she has been asked this question many times before. I turn to our other friend for the truth… "It's sheep's stomach lining, stuffed with stuff." I can sense she thinks it's better to just say "stuff" than to tell me the details. But I persist and as it turns out, I should have let the sleeping sheep sleep because this is what I learn… "Haggis is sheep's "pluck" (heart, liver and lungs) minced with onion, oatmeal, suet (the hard, white fat on the kidneys and loins), spices and salt, mixed with stock, traditionally encased in the animal's stomach," she quotes as if right from Wikipedia.

Yum?

Oh my. Nothing about this sounds delicious. It sounds the opposite of delicious. I take a deep breath and prepare my order. Hey, when in Rome… So I try the haggis prepared three different ways. The first, I dislike. The second, I really dislike! But the third, oh the third, I really, really, *really* dislike. It has a pasty texture that I think only a mother could love.

Ah well, I gave it a fair shot. Next up on the menu is a Scotch Egg. Slightly worried but committed to the plan, I dive in.

I really try not to use the word *hate*. I learned this from my son when he was a teen. He said, "I hate Justin Bieber. Wait, I don't really hate him, actually I don't even know him. I hate his music. No wait, hate is too strong a word for music, I should save the word hate for truly awful things like war and murder." Smart kid. Now I hardly ever use the word hate. What word could you get rid of?

This deep fried, sausage encrusted, hard-boiled egg may sound like a breakfast food but it's not. It needs neither mustard or ketchup and it is, in fact, quite delicious. Probably not terribly nutritious but yummy!

Speaking of not too nutritious, the last thing on the menu is the Deep Fried Mars Bar. And while it's a tough job, I am willing to take one for the team and it's all I can do not to lick my plate. Mmm, mmm, good.

I was happy that I tried the haggis more than one time. Too often we make judgements and decision based on one time, one way. Trying a variety of different options helped me be pretty sure that there is no Scottish blood in my lineage.

These three items from the pub launch my challenge to try fifty new foods. I don't think I'm much different than most North Americans who generally buy the same twenty-five foods over and over again. We typically prepare the same twelve meals over and over again, and when we go out we often order similar meals over and over again. Chicken fingers, anyone?

With this new challenge in my back pocket grocery shopping is a little more exciting, meal preparation is a little more stimulating and eating out is a little more of an adventure. Everything related to food is, in fact, a wee bit different, which is nice. The menus seem to be smaller as I mentally cancel out so many of the old standbys I was used to having.

A partial list of my *Please Pass Me Some More* now includes:

Persimmon, White Sweet Potato, Lagneh, Conk Salad, Tadiq, Hush Puppies, and Mullet.

A few foods on my list of *If I'm Super Hungry I'll Force 'Em Down* are: Boudin Balls, Acorn Squash, and Grits.

Making my *Please Don't Ever Make Me Eat These Again* list are: Cassava, Sardines, Boiled Peanuts, Cricket Powder and of course, Haggis!

Taste is a very personal thing. Don't let others sway you; try it yourself!

Your taste buds change as you age. What you didn't like before you may find you have a hankering for now! Maybe you simply didn't like the way it was prepared last time, as was the case with The Hub. For twenty years he told me he didn't like mashed potatoes and he refused to taste them. When he finally acquiesced and tried my mom's it turned out it he liked them quite a lot! Maybe it wasn't that he didn't like mashed potatoes, maybe he just didn't like *his* mom's mashed potatoes. (Sorry Jeannette!) Gasp!

Wake up your taste buds, shock them, stimulate them, thrill them by trying something new. Applying *The Try Angle* to food, you will find that sometimes you'll love it, sometimes you won't, and sometimes you will find a week's worth of calories in one delicious item and it will be worth every single calorie!

Try 5

may the force be with you

THERE IS a tool called the Wheel of Life that we coaches love to use to assess life balance. I used it now and again for self-assessment and in my work with clients. No matter what season of life I was in, when I did this assessment I always came up short in the same area–spirituality.

Spirituality has always been lacking for me. Raised a church-going Roman Catholic, even teaching Sunday School to little ones as a teenager, I was constantly envying those who were so faithful, so devout, so certain. I felt jealous, wanting something they had but unsure how to make it happen. I was living in confusion and I had wanted to work on this at some point in time.

Now is the time. I sign up for three sessions of spiritual counselling. I have no idea what to expect, but three sessions seems like a Kaizen amount–enough to get an understanding but not too much to overwhelm.

Tracy, my guide, helps me understand that spirituality takes many different forms, some as obvious and didactic as religion, some more subtle, as in showing patience or seeking answers to questions that we didn't know we had. She helps me see that spirit works through me and in me when I am doing my work and living my life. She says that the good I do is indeed spirit. I'd never thought about it that way. The Hub and I make a commitment to continue to nurture a spirit of kindness and generosity in each other. We write on the bathroom mirror in dry erase marker as a daily reminder that we each have different ways of being kind and generous to each other and to the world and neither is right or wrong. For example, he is an extremely generous tipper. I tip, but not to the same extent, and I know that I have made him feel bad for giving too much money in the past when in fact, I should have been supporting him in his effort to be kind and generous. Conversely, I am very generous with my time and he would sometimes make me feel bad for helping people and taking time away from us to do so. Renewing our commitment to nurture a spirit of kindness and generosity in our many forms has really helped us solidify this branch of spirituality.

The other take away from my spirituality coaching was learning to focus on discernment–the space between making a decision and having a decision made. Being comfortable with the not knowing. As an impatient type, I did need to practice being okay with not knowing. It wasn't that the answer wasn't coming at all; it was about learning to be okay with knowing that the answer just had not come yet.

Like a plane that has taken off but not yet landed, it is somewhere in between, not lost–just in transition. It has departed, but has not yet arrived. Allowing spirit to work in the space in between seems to be a good practice to implement.

I no longer envy those that have a different type of religion or spirituality than I do. I seek to learn from them and understand more, and I now have a new appreciation of where my own spirituality integrates into my life.

Could I have done this on my own? Maybe, but I hadn't up until the point that I committed to utilizing the skills of a coach–even coaches need coaches, you know. Her fresh perspective was great and proved valuable on many fronts, and now that the door is open a crack the light is coming in.

Try 6

note to self

WHEN I SPEAK, coach and consult, people often look to me for answers. I sure don't have them all but I guess I wouldn't be doing what I'm doing if I didn't have a few. For this challenge I wondered what it would be like if I advised myself (and the world via my Facebook page). After 50 days of inspiration practice I discovered these little vignettes of awareness that I still use today.

Notes to Self:

1. Not everyone wants to hear my message.
2. Fudge tastes better when scraped from the sides of the pot.
3. Sitting by a fire is good for the soul.
4. If you see something good, say something good.
5. Just because some is good, it doesn't mean more is better.
6. Treat people like beloved family members.
7. When you do good, you get good. Sometimes it's right away, sometimes it just takes awhile.
8. A good night's sleep makes everything a little easier.
9. When people want to help you, let them.
10. Buy based on value, not cost.
11. No one can love you like your mommy can.

12. Certainty hampers growth.

13. Music makes me happy.

14. Perfection is highly overrated.

15. Sometimes there is a fine line between the things I want and the things I need.

16. Home is where my honey is.

17. There is usually more than one right answer.

18. If you don't have it, you can't give it.

19. Choose to invest in people who choose to invest in me.

20. Nature doesn't need me, but I need nature.

21. I can't help other people feel happy unless I feel happy.

22. My health is my #1 business and I will have no business if I have no health.

23. It's never too late or too early to say thanks. (Inspired by an audience member who sent me a "free hugs" change purse as a thank you years after hearing me speak.)

24. Setbacks can be temporary.

25. The little things are the big things.

26. I can do something today that will make me a better person tomorrow.

27. My time is finite; the things people want from me are infinite. I have to set boundaries to stay sane.

28. I don't have to know how I'm going to get there, I just have to start moving in the right direction.

29. From sunscreen to condoms, health insurance to helmets, some things are for your protection. Use them with gratitude.

30. Leave things better than you found them.

31. I can learn something from everyone. Everyone.

32. Radiate what you want to receive.

33. Using words like never and always are usually incorrect.

34. Be gentle, everyone is going through something.

35. Pay it forward is not just the name of a movie, it's a way of life.

36. Investing in experiences is rarely a waste of money, resources or effort.

37. Watching people you love do something they love is an incredible high.

38. Monday can be just as great a day as Friday. It's your choice.

39. You're never lost; you're just not there yet.

40. Love, affection and appreciation can be delivered to you in all sorts of atypical ways.

41. No matter what your head wants to do, your body, health, or lack thereof, wins.

42. If I don't learn something from every experience or interaction, it's my own fault.

43. Anticipation is half the fun!

44. Some things you start cannot be undone. Once you know, you cannot "unknow." What you experience, you cannot "un-experience." Once you see you cannot "unsee." Once you feel, you cannot "unfeel."

45. More stuff equals more stress.

46. Other people challenging you is generally more challenging than challenging yourself.

49. Ideas are great, but it's the execution that matters more.

50. Privilege blinds.

51. If it's not delicious and it's not healthy, don't eat it.

52. If there are stairs, take them!

53. Stop at lemonade stands, toy stores and scenic lookouts. Candy stores should not be passed by either, just poke your head in for a nostalgic peek. (As it so happens I am stopped in the middle of my three hour road trip at a little lake and am writing. The sun is shining, the birds are chirping, a warm breeze is blowing and the geese and goslings are puttering around. It's divine.)

It seems I surpassed 50, but I so enjoyed doing this challenge because it forced me to find the good in whatever situation arose that particular day. It allowed me to be creatively grateful and it increased my awareness of what was happening around me.

You might want to try it. Whether you post it publicly or on a sticky note by your computer or, my personal favorite, with a dry erase marker on the bathroom mirror, it's a cool, inspiring challenge.

Try 7

music to my ears

THIS CHALLENGE happened by accident while I was pressing the station buttons in my car. It took me to 107.1 FM, our local classical radio station.

My first inclination is to change the station and find something I like, something more "me." Then that familiar shift happens and I know that I will be immersing myself in classical music, for well, the next fifty days, of course.

It is a bit of a shock at first. Every time I start the ignition in my car and hear the music I am surprised by the unfamiliar welcoming.

On one of the first evenings, the full moon rises and glows and clouds breeze before the giant ball creating a magical picture, I wonder if I would have enjoyed and appreciated this idyllic scene as much–or would have even noticed it–had I been singing along to my favourite top forty tunes instead of listening to Mozart's *Clarinet Concerto in A*. Maybe. Maybe not.

As the days pass, I notice how the music makes me feel. Some of it makes me sad while some of it makes me want to drive faster. Other times, it makes me think this is a stupid project.

Some of the music makes me wonder. Some of it makes me happy. Some it is familiar, but most of it is not. One of the most significant things I notice is that none of the music has words which means no singing from me. It forces me to keep my mouth shut and listen. What a good skill for a speaker to practice!

Trying to decipher the instruments is another fascination–is it a flute or a pan flute? For all I know about instruments it could have been a pot flute. Maybe it's that clarinet again, I just don't know.

In the middle of this challenge, The Hub and I, after thirty-three years of going on dates, decide to have a date night like we have never had before. We decide to go to a symphony. The promotions for the Winnipeg Symphony Orchestra with guest conductor Rainer Hersch bragged about the fun factor of this particular event.

Though doubtful, we lay down our credit card, invite some other virgin symphony-going friends, dress up all "perty-like" and enter the concert hall trying to fit in but not at all convinced this is a good use of our time or money.

Much to our delight, from the moment the talented comedian/conductor stumbles onto the stage, our first symphony experience turns out to be so much fun–full of audience interaction, silliness, and loads of laughing. Leading a two-hour performance, Mr. Hersch combines his two unique gifts, music and comedy, to bring the stage to life. I think he makes each one of us, whether we are musically inclined or not, feel connected to what is going on up on that stage.

The learning from this Try? What for decades we had prejudged to be a stuffy, boring event was anything but, leaving me with sore cheeks from laughing and The Hub and our symphony-virgin friends pleasantly surprised with the enjoyment we experienced.

As for the radio station, while pop, rock or new country is still a staple in the Staples' vehicles, we are no longer afraid of, or do we shy away from classical, and we happily include it in the mix every now and then!

Try 8

the fitness challenge

Isn't it fun when some people seem more into your project than you are! Kassy Bouchard, who has been my personal trainer for many years now, is like that. Once a week, when I am not on the road speaking, I make my way into her gym where we workout together.

It's 6:30 a.m. and I charge into the gym with all the enthusiasm that a morning workout brings–you can imagine, can't you?

The very authentic Kassy greets me with a big smile. "I've got a special workout for you today!" "Oh goodie," I say, not sure if I am serious or joking.

I see her challenge written in dry erase marker on the mirror of the gym.

It says:

- 50 sit-ups
- 50 Russian twists
- 50 squats
- 50 curls
- 50 calf raises
- 50 chin-ups
- 50 deadlifts
- 50 burpees
- 50 pulley leg kickbacks
- 50 tricep push ups

Suddenly my smile goes away. "Fifty of each?" I ask incredulously. "All today?"

"Yep, and I'm going to do it too," she says, like that's supposed to make me feel better. Um, she's twenty something–did I mention I'm 50?

"Is this negotiable?" I ask. "How about I do your age and you do mine, that seems reasonable?"

Nope, this does not seem to be up for negotiation.

So we start. I turn it into a game. "How many can I do? In which order should I do them?" I pick up the dry erase marker to track my progress. Oh, it feels good to check off those exercises, even if it's just five or ten at a time. Apparently we release a little hit of endorphins when we check things off a list!

Some feel easy, for example the sit-ups. Some seem impossible–who the heck can do fifty chin-ups? Does she mean this year? I can do fifty chin ups this year, I think.

Nonetheless, Kassy is patient and she says I can take my time, but it's clear I'm not allowed to leave until I have completed my challenge.

I huff and I puff. I grunt and I groan. Sometime later that day I finish and it feels amazing. I am 50 and even if the scale does not tell me what I want to hear, I know that for the most part I am fit, strong and healthy. Really, what more can a girl, or a woman of my advanced age, ask for?

From this Try I learned that taking your time, adapting the rules and charting your progress are all very viable ways to bring your goals to fruition. Right from the start, imagining how you will feel upon completion really helps. Noticing how far you have come, as opposed to lamenting about how far you have to go, is a much more positive way to look at things. Perhaps most importantly, sometimes other people believe in you more than you believe in yourself, and sometimes their certainty is strong enough to help you overcome your doubt.

Sometimes you get to be the cheerleader and sometimes you get to be cheered on and both can be equally cool.

Try 9

the silent partnership

WE AREN'T having a fight and we aren't mad at each other. We just don't speak for twenty-four hours in a row and it is hard!

It all started as we walked the beach on our holidays, chatting mindlessly about nothing in particular, without a care in the world.

I don't know how it came up or even remember whose idea it was, although I'm quite sure most people would point to me. I'm not 100% certain, but one of us said it out loud… "I wonder what it would be like if we didn't speak for twenty-four hours?"

Thus began a fascinating conversation about the idea of communicating without words during a day that we would be together for every minute. The Hub thinks it will be easy, maybe because he is, after all, the quiet one in our relationship. I know it will be hard. We agree to start spontaneously right then and there on the beach with no forethought or preparations. We just look at the time and give the nod–10 a.m. to 10 a.m. Go!

It feels weird from the get-go, strolling without so much as a peep being exchanged. This self-enforced silence feels very unnatural. Lots of uncommon facial expressions and grand gestures are being used to replace the words we would have used. The odd time one of us forgets and starts to talk. Sometimes we forget that we can talk to other people–that's funny.

At 10 a.m. the next day we can't shut up, we are so excited to debrief–what we had thought, how we had felt, how hard it was, what we missed, and what we liked.

We both noted many things from this brief experience:

- We thought a lot more. This seemed ironic as I imagined talking would provoke thought. I guess this explains why the gurus want us to be in silence much more often.

- We felt like people were looking at us while we were doing things like grocery shopping. Did we look like a couple who was deaf? How did that make us feel?

- There sure were a lot of things we (okay, probably mostly me) would have said that were unimportant and really didn't matter.

- When things were really important we tried very hard to communicate our message and we got frustrated when the other person didn't understand us no matter how hard we tried.

- We noticed how much more important touch was; we wanted to connect physically even more when the words were absent. (After this, we also tried twenty-four hours with not touching. That was very interesting indeed!)

Whether you have been together "forever" or are a new couple, we would both recommend The Silent Partnership challenge.

What we didn't know at the time was that this unconventional Try would be far from the strangest thing we would do this year.

Try 10

parkour

PARKOUR—do you know it? No, Okay, Google says:

parkour / pär'k͞oor / *noun*: The activity or sport of moving rapidly through an area, typically in an urban environment, negotiating obstacles by running, jumping and climbing.

If you have not seen this sport demonstrated before, it will be worth a quick search before you read on. Go ahead, I'll wait...

I can't remember how I discovered it but the moment I saw it I was enthralled. It's pretty impressive to see these young, agile, mostly male, athletic types leap, hop, skip, jump and somersault over everything in their paths, along with some out of the way obstacles too.

Most people would think that those teens are a little off their rockers and that what they are doing is nothing that someone in the second half of their life should be attempting.

I am enthralled with this parkour and I know that we don't always have to jump in with both feet, sometimes we just have to get creative as to how to put a toe in. How could I Kaizen this activity, amp up my activity level a bit and not kill myself in the process?

I certainly could not do what these young bucks were doing. I imagine they must have had a background in gymnastics the way they were moving about. However, there was something I could do and it started with seeing my surroundings differently.

From that moment on, every walk I go on presented me with obstacles—the good kind of obstacles! Benches, curbs, posts, low fences, large rocks all call out to me, "Climb me, jump off me, balance on

me, bounce off of me, use me"… and so I do! There is no doubt in my mind that I look ridiculous. I remind myself that it is none of my business what people who don't know me, care about me or love me–people that for the most part I will never see again–think about me. The time to stop caring about what those people think is right now. This very minute. Stop it. So I do because I'm having fun. I'm turning boring old walks and runs into creative challenges and burning more calories at the same time. I'm hooked!

I discover that in Toronto there is a parkour gym where they give lessons, so on my next trip I decide to enhance my parkour skills. I phone the gym to inquire–yes they give lessons, no there is no age limit, and yes, there is something they can teach "older" people. Okay… I'm in.

We all know things are more fun with a friend, so I enlist Barbara, my 56-year-old marathon running friend—she will be perfect! We book a private class for just the two of us with instructor Kyle (who appears to be about twelve years old). Kyle is fantastic. Not once does he laugh at us even though we stumble, fumble and ask him to repeat the instructions as many times as we do.

When our lesson is over we are invited to stay and "play" in the studio. Yes, we are the only women there and yes we are the only ones over twenty there as well. I ask the boys what they like about the sport and they hammer out, "Strength, agility, trust, power, progressive learning, compound activities." They have been trained well. Even though each one has a war wound to show for the sport (a bad shoulder, a bad back, a bum wrist) they are enthusiasts to their core and it is contagious!

I have noticed that pilots, surgeons, bankers and pretty much all professionals are only about twelve years old these days. I realize that this is a reflection of the fact that I am getting older not that they are getting younger. Unfortunately.

When Barbara steps out to make a call, I take advantage of the situation and climb into the advanced area. (She should know that I shouldn't be left unattended!) Without my trusty friend to ground me, I somehow end up atop a really high plank. Getting up is challenging enough, but getting down proves to be the biggest challenge of the day.

Barbara throws her head into her hands in shock when she sees me high up in the rafters of the gym listening to the young boy trying to coax me down. It seems I have two options. I can walk across a railway tie-like beam that is too many feet above the ground, then jump down to a lower level and leap across my plank to another one that is way too far away for my short legs, limited skills and advanced age. Or I can jump straight down. Umm. Neither of these options seem particularly enticing.

After much too long trying to decide, the boy drags two huge mattresses, demonstrates twice how to jump and land, and after much fanfare and coaxing, with my heart racing in irrational fear, I jump.

"Hey, that's fun, can I do it again?"

Parkour–it's not just for young people anymore!

$\mathcal{T}ry\ 11$

the carrot in front of my nose

WE SAW IT on *Dragon's Den*, the *Shark Tank*-like show where entrepreneurs pitch their products hoping to snag an investor to take their product to the next level. They called themselves Daisy Cakes, and using an old family recipe, and an entire pound of carrots in each cake, they presented a carrot cake that wowed each and every investor. Ever since we watched that episode years ago, I had a secret desire to surprise my carrot cake loving husband with one. Try as I might, year after year, I wasn't able get the cake delivered to Canada.

Finally a great opportunity presents itself and I decide to implement my great carrot cake plan. I will be away from home for business for numerous weeks and The Hub and I will be meeting in Portland for a couple's retreat (that's another story altogether) in between all the travel for work. What if I get the cake delivered there as a surprise?

I phone the hotel to ensure that they can receive the cake and care for it until we arrive. Then I phone Daisy Cakes to order. I'm so excited! It is all going well until the cake guy tells me the amount that will be charged to my credit card... $89. Yikes. That would be U.S. dollars to boot, which would make it about kajillion dollars Canadian. (Okay it is actually $138–but still!)

I am prepared for the $50 cake but I have not taken into account the extreme delivery charge for such a fragile item. By this point though, I have already gone to so much trouble and I can practically visualize presenting him with his surprise, so I gulp and put the order through.

When we arrive at the hotel, the cake is beyond perfect!

Packed in a cooler with dry ice, it is huge and heavy in a beautifully branded tin. As a surprise bonus (since *obviously* we are celebrating something with a cake, I guess) the hotel upgrades our room, places the cake on the desk and leaves us a free bottle of wine.

The Hub is surprised and thrilled. Every day for the four days of our little holiday we enjoy the best carrot cake we have ever tasted. In fact, we eat so much I'm pretty sure we never need carrot cake again!

Was I crazy to pay this amount of money for a cake? Maybe. Then again maybe not. Somebody on my Facebook feed thought so though. She thought it was a terrible use of money and pointed out that I could have/should have used that money in much better ways, donating it to the needy perhaps.

Of course I could have, but I stand by my decision. I do many philanthropic things and this was not one of them. I did not pay $138 for a cake, I paid $138 for an experience. I paid to surprise my main man, to create a memory, and to quench the desire for something we had been wanting for a long time.

I paid to celebrate our reunion and Valentine's Day and the fact that after thirty-three years together we were doing a couple's retreat–how cool is that! I paid because for two decades we'd saved and did the "right thing" with the little bit of money we had. I paid $138 because I could, because we are at a time in our lives when that hard work has paid off and we have some play money. I paid because we are generous with others and do good for people and causes all the time, and we deserve to treat ourselves to an indulgence every once in a while.

So, I indulged. I paid $138 for a cake and an experience that was worth every penny and bite.

Now it's your turn–what do you deserve to indulge in? Try it!

This reminds me of a friend who was biking home from the grocery store with her goods in her basket. She stopped to offer a man who appeared homeless a banana. He took it and then noticed the pear in her cart and he asked for the pear. She really wanted the pear and she only had one so she said, "No." She didn't know whether to feel good or bad about stopping to share. Similarly, I was leaving a downtown restaurant with a half of a vegetarian burrito and a cookie in tow. I noticed someone one the street corner and I said, "You can have the cookie or the burrito, but not both." He laughed and choose the cookie. Are we kind for stopping to share or selfish for not giving more? You may judge. I think sometimes we give what we have, sometimes we give what we want and sometimes we don't give at all. In any case, giving with a happy heart trumps giving any other way.

$\mathcal{T}ry$ 12

the exsweariment

I GIVE MYSELF permission to try swearing in my outside voice. I am a little nervous about letting the expletives out of my lips, because even as a teen I never swore at home and very, very rarely outside of home either. I made no judgement about swearing, except for the people whose every second word is F^*#, I have no patience for that. I just never felt like "I should" (good girls don't, etc.). When we started our family it seemed to be a no-brainer to remove the swears completely from my vocabulary. The Hub was not a habitual swearer, he reserved his for very choice moments and thus we ended up with three very nice, polite, non-swearing children. (Although they never swore in front of us, I am not so naive as to think they didn't swear at all.)

Anyway…

I don't know and I can't really explain why, but suddenly I just feel the need to play with these previously self-forbidden words. Even while typing, such a good girl was I that I would type *wth*, instead of–gasp–*wtf*. F that (gasp again). My fingers even feel bad typing those three letters in succession! Now I feel done with censoring; the kids are in their early twenties and I feel like once in a while it will be okay, under the proper circumstances, to let one out. A swear word that is.

Although feeling foreign on my tongue, I begin the exsweariment.

It doesn't go all that well. I should have guessed it would be a shock for the kids. They are definitely taken aback. They hadn't ever heard me swear. (Can I please get a point for twenty years of never

Wtf is that—a spontaneous explosion of happiness? lol *Exsweariment!* I just made that up this moment, sitting here at O'Hare. Is it just me or is that a perfect word for this? I invented a new word; I am doing a happy dance in my head! Do you ever just get a thought or an idea and you are like, "Heh, that's clever, brilliant, awesome, funny, etc." And you think, "Who thought of that?" and then you're like, "Me!!" And you get to be clever, brilliant, awesome and funny. Sometimes you are the only one that thinks so, but that's okay. "It's my word and this is my moment, let me enjoy it." *Exsweariment*—I just went and registered it in the Urban Dictionary—yep I did! Next time you invent a word, throw it in there, it's a little rush!

letting my kids hear me swear? Even I'm impressed!).

"Mommmmmmmm, what are you doing????? You don't swear!" said my Middle-est, who can't believe her ears and is the spokesperson for the trio.

"I just thought I would try it out." I say, without the slightest bit of defensiveness.

"Mommmmmm, you can't just not swear your whole life and suddenly start swearing!!!!!"

"Why not?" I ask with every morsel of seriousness I can muster. "It's not like I didn't swear before, I just didn't swear out loud before. I swore a lot in my head."

"We may be grown up but we still need role models," she whines without missing a beat.

Oh shit, seriously? They are all grown up and I still have to watch my words. F*^# that. ;)

I'm just kidding. No, I'm not. Actually, this is about more than me watching my vocabulary. This is about allowing my kids, my world, myself to see and experience the whole me—well, at least a bigger part of me than they had seen or experienced before. It's time to stop apologizing for being who I am. I am a person that swears sometimes. Sue me.

I am inspired to write about other things that I am tired of apologizing for and the result is this Slam Poem. In case this is new to you, *Slam Poetry is an introspective and creative spoken word art that is performed with a tad of sass, drama and style. It is moving people across the globe.*

I Apologize
I'm sorry if I forgot your birthday or your anniversary
If I picked you up late or too early for the show
I apologize, if I offended in some way, either unintentionally
Or maybe, if I was having a bad day, I was intentionally mean
I apologize if you didn't feel included
If you were secluded
And I didn't open my arms to you
I apologize whether you are a friend or a stranger
Whether you have been in my life a little or a lot
If you felt I hurt you in any way forgive me, hear that true and
	sincere
But... forgive me not
Because I don't apologize, I won't apologize for being me,
Human, flawed, imperfect
I tried to conform but it wasn't worth it
I make no more apologies for my sensitive nature
For crying at O Canada or not reading the newspaper
I hear the news everywhere, I don't need to stare at the
	crumbling buildings
The people dying and guns blasting, I know it's happening
I make no apologies because it hurts too much, so I just do
	what I can
For my fellow man, here, right where I stand
In little ways that might not seem to matter much
But I do it anyway. Because I can. Because I care.

And, I won't apologize for the age I am, it's mine to own
The colour of my skin, or the size of my grin
I won't apologize for being an extrovert, it's who I am
I make no apologies for my looks, for my Italian nose,
My extra long toes, they are in fact the only long and slender
    part of me
"Where are your legs?" my 'friend' asked as she was walking up
    the stairs behind me
I laughed, but I hurt, I make no more apologies for what God
    gave me
My stature, my nature, my eccentric behaviour.
I do apologize if I wronged you, hear that true and sincere
But my dear
I make no apologies for the way that I sneeze
My wrinkles or knees
And especially for my sometimes excessive, overly positive
    outlook
That may annoy you but I can't destroy you
When I come from a place of love and hope and good intention
So if I forgot to mention
I make no apologies for who I am
Failed, flawed and hopelessly human.
What will you not apologize for?

Try 13

pull up a couch

I GET OUT of my car to read the street sign that had fallen over. It is a dark and starry night, about 9 p.m. when I turn down the road with no street lights, guided by my GPS, to this quaint little Florida town called St. Augustine.

I am slightly nervous pulling up for my first couch surfing experience and I leave my bags in the car, just in case I don't get a "good vibe" from my hosts. Tentatively, I knock on the door and am immediately welcomed by wagging tails and warm hugs which quickly dissipates my worry.

This particular Try, given to me by my world travelling, adventurous friend Tony Esteves, is to couch surf. CouchSurfing International Inc. started in 2003 and espouses these values: sharing ones life, creating connections, staying curious, offering kindness, and leaving the world better than you found it, all things I can stand behind with a big smile on my face!

As a seasoned traveller for both business and pleasure, I have my share of frequent flyer miles and hotel loyalty cards. But never in my travels had I considered couch surfing; I didn't, in fact, clearly understand what it was. When Tony, an experienced "surfer" brought it to my attention, my first thought was that I might be thirty years too old to be doing this. But I wasn't. As I soon learned, there are couch surfers much older than I am using this service to experience the world.

It's hard to believe that no money–yep, you read that correctly–no money changes hands during this exchange. People (many of whom are seasoned travellers themselves) open their homes to help others and for the experience of getting to know and learn from them. Ideally, it is less about saving money and more about creating cool exchanges. So, even though my client was happily paying my travel costs for the four-city Florida speaking tour, I decided to surf.

Back to my St. Augustine hosts… and what I haven't mentioned yet. Before I head over to their house, I go to the beach. I see huge rocks jutting out to into the ocean. Are these breakwaters? I don't know what they are but to me they look like a great place to do some yoga poses. So I find a nice flat rock and take in the sights, smells and sounds that the ocean offers, and enjoy stillness, calm and centering that yoga poses afford. And then… *squirrel!*

I know what these rocks would be great for! Parkour!! Oh my gosh–these would be amazing obstacles for Parkour!

Goodbye yoga! I begin bouncing my way down the rocks, delighting in the thrill of my newfound accomplishment. Parkour in the ocean, who wouldn't want to do this?!

"It's all fun until someone loses an eye." Isn't that how the expression goes?

I skip and bop in complete happiness until, like the bad part in a movie, everything seems to be happening in *s l o w   m o t i o n …*

One rock is full of algae. Wet algae. Do I need to tell you that wet algae is slippery? I see it too late, my foot is already landing on that exact rock and I start to slip. I'm sure it happened in a nanosecond but it felt like it took a long time because the slo-mo kicked in. I could see exactly where my head was going to hit… a sharp jagged rock. "This is not going to be good."

Immediately my sunglasses go flying and a curtain of bright red blood floods my face. Uh-oh.

With nobody in sight, I know I have to get myself back to the beach in a hurry to get help. Thankfully, two young moms see me; they rush over with a towel in hand and have me sit with them to recuperate a bit. (Their poor children were probably traumatized by this bleeding stranger crashing their beach party.)

Insisting I'm "fine" and don't need them to call anyone, I try to make my way back to my car. I guess it's no surprise that they let me keep their blood-drenched towel.

As I make my way down the beach (it seems much further than when I walked the other way) many people stop to a offer help or ask if they can call someone for me.

I am adamant that I am "fine", but by the time I reach the board-walk that leads to my car I meet my match and this lovely lady lets me

See, I believe people are inherently good, that most people want to do good and help and make the world a better place. I genuinely believe this and overall it has served me well. I really, really love living life that way.

go no further. Soon I hear sirens and fire trucks and for the first time in my life, they are for me. Sigh.

It is quite a big production, to stitch or not to stitch. They say to stitch, I say, "Nah, I got this, I used to be a nurse." So in the end, after they ensure I am in my right mind (Ha–I fooled them; I am rarely in a "right mind" state!) I wander over to the nearby pharmacy to assess the damage I had done to myself. It is not pretty at all, perhaps I should have stitched. Too late! I buy myself some steri-strips to put the gash in my head back together and I clean up as best I can.

If you do not have steri-strips in your medicine cabinet and travel bag, I highly suggest you get some–they are little medical miracles that put gashes that are not quite bad enough for stitches, back together. While you are at the pharmacy to stock your medicine cabinet and suitcase may I also suggest you purchase some medical paper tape? This is also a Godsend. Put it on your toes if you are prone to blisters, redness, corns, or rubbing of any kind. It will act like a second skin and really help to avoid/lessen the irritation. You can thank me later.

Next I head off to meet a speaking colleague. I have only met Pegine Echevarria, a highly respected and successful entrepreneur, online and she kindly offered to spend some time with me while I was in her area. I am eager to be in her presence and I'm not going to let this little incident make me miss out. I think I should give her a heads up though–pardon the pun–because I'm not exactly looking like my profile picture and I don't want her to be too shocked when she sees me. This sweet lady shows up with a whole bag filled with bandages, gauze and alcohol (not the drinking kind). I suspect neither of us will ever forget our first meeting; it was quite memorable!

Following our wonderful time together it is time for me to head off to meet my first couch surfing hosts, and that's where you came in at the beginning of the chapter. What I didn't tell you then is that I arrived at their place with bandages on my head, my hair full of dried blood, and quite possibly more than a little concussed. There is some irony in that; as I mentioned at the beginning of this story, I was a bit afraid of what my couch surfing hosts would be like, but most likely upon greeting me, they were more afraid than I was!

Still this young, adventurous couple who had welcomed other guests from around the world into their home, welcome me in as well. Not for money, just to bring a bit more of the world into their lives.

When I am leaving them after two lovely nights at their place, they say, "You know Steph, when you went to bed that first night, we sat out here thinking, "God, I hope she doesn't die in that room, that would look so bad on our couch surfing profile!" I laugh and confess to them what had been going through my mind that night, "I hope I don't die in this room, that would look very bad on their CouchSurfing profile!" I could just envision it, "Come stay with us, most people leave alive."

In just a few short days, thanks to CouchSurfing, I stay with a couple who had lived on a boat for a year, along with a hula-hooping waitress who is studying to be a Naturopathic Doctor and gives me a private poolside yoga lesson. I enjoy a homemade Indian meal with a couple who have only been in the country for one year, and I have a full day motorcycle tour with a man who has cycled across America. All of the people I meet tell me story after story of great experiences they have had both being hosts and surfers. You just don't get these kind of experiences at the Hampton. (But Hampton, I do love your five o'clock, not-from-the-oven chocolate chip cookies.)

You also don't get to know people like this if you assume everyone is out to get you.

Oh, and if you are wondering about the whole "couch" thing, while some hosts do have couches for their guests in a shared space, all of my experiences included a private room. You just have to read the profiles well to make sure you understand what is available to you and, of course, do your due diligence when checking out profiles and references. Safety rules and common sense should prevail; intuition and inklings should be followed. If you are interested in learning about how other people live (and saving a boatload of money in the process), I highly encourage you to burst the hotel bubble this year and learn to surf!

Meanwhile, it's time to pay it forward. Our shingle is out and our almost empty nest is open for traveling birds who are passing through. So far our experiences as CouchSurfing hosts have been great!

Maybe our next guest will be... you!

Try 14

without you

I WAS GOING to be away on a Monday-to-Friday business trip and somehow this idea unfolded... what if The Hub and I don't communicate for that entire length of time? No calls, no texts, no email, no Skype. All of the things that help us stay connected when we are miles apart we would voluntarily give up for five days. The Hub would be working all day and taking a course every evening, and I would be working and traveling, so we would both be very busy.

We both thought this would probably be a pretty easy challenge to pull off as we had done well with our twenty-four hours of silence challenge. How hard could this be? In fact, we thought it might even make things easier. Now we were free to really focus on where we were and who we were with and let our minds be strictly in the present moment.

I would like to take a moment to thank my beloved for supporting me on all these odd thoughts I have, and especially for willingly joining in on so many!

From the very first day we know it is going to be much harder than we had originally anticipated. We both have very tough weeks which doesn't help–I put out my back and end up in the ER, The Hub is having a challenging time in his course. Without each other to lean on, even if only with Skype, text, email, or phone, we both feel lost, lonely, and sad. It turns out neither of us use this time to amp up our other relationships (which may have been a smart thing to do) we just suffer in silence. On Thursday I cue up a text exclaiming, "I hate this!" which I don't end up sending. We have made it through this experiment for four days and I only have to wait one more day.

By the time he picks me up from the airport on Friday night we are both so cranky! Cranky and grateful. We agree we are never doing this experiment again and we talk about why it was so hard. We agree that we did not have that special person to debrief with about our respective days, our chief commiserator when things were spiralling downhill, and our champion when we had a win to share. During our twenty-four hours of silence we could still see each other, feel each other, share space and air and energy. This week we had none of that. It was as if the other person had disappeared and we didn't like that.

The lesson was a new appreciation for how important those avenues of communication are with the ones we love. We gained a new appreciation of how much we count on each other even when, perhaps especially when, we are apart, for support and comfort and sharing. We have a new appreciation of what it would be like without the other person there waiting for us, being our number one fan.

We had a renewed appreciation for each other.

Try 15

the ukulele lady

My brothers are self-taught, amazing guitarists. I grew up with bands practicing in the basement, instruments, amps and cords strewn everywhere. I looked longingly at those precious pieces, I listened and watched, secretly wanting to be part of that world.

When I was a teen I got my first (and only) guitar. I loved looking at it, I loved holding it, I loved hearing its strings collaborate into a song I recognized. I tried and tried to make the guitar sing like my brothers could. I practiced basic chords until my fingers ached. I played that guitar until it was out of tune but I couldn't for the life of me tune it. I just couldn't figure it out. Maybe I didn't inherit an ear for music because, even with an electric tuner, I couldn't figure it out.

I kept my guitar for a few years, every once in a while picking it up and letting my fingers magically fall into the right places. Eventually looking at the guitar didn't make me happy, it made me sad. Every time I saw it I thought I had failed, that I wasn't good, and I couldn't do it. I felt sorry for myself and I even felt sorry for my guitar because neither of us were living up to our potential. Not only was my guitar not singing, my guitar gently wept. .

Finally, I made a decision. Clearly many people played music, but there also had to be people who *appreciated* music. Since I obviously did not have the aptitude to be a musician, I would become the best appreciator of music and musicians that I could be. This shift of mindset really helped me decide that it was time to give my guitar away, to let it out of its misery and give it to someone who could make it sing.

A couple of short decades later, the 50/50 List and *The Try Angle* change all that. I challenge myself to learn an instrument. Maybe a harmonica, I think. It's portable, fun and it will be cool around the campfire! Worst case scenario I will get a tambourine–everyone can play a tambourine!

But then I see her, she's like a cross between Aunt Jemima and the Chiquita Banana lady (you may have to be 50+ to know what I'm talking about here). Suffice it to say she is dressed in blue with a headpiece that would cause her to duck through most doorways. She enters the stage with flourish carrying a little teeny tiny guitar. It is a ukulele and she is *The Ukulele Lady* and I can't take my eyes off of her. I haven't seen anything like this before. Lana Bullough, one of my professional speaking colleagues, has this oft-hidden alter ego and on this evening, the Canadian Association of Professional Speakers (CAPS) is going to find out about it! The first *CAPS Got Talent* night will showcase members who have talents beyond speaking.

The Ukulele Lady positions herself on the stool in the middle of

"While My Guitar Gently Weeps"–a bow to the Beatles for another stellar song. My brother was a Beatles fan and I can still see the albums lined up like library books in his room. I can hear the music flow up the vents from his room to mine. I bet I know practically every lyric to almost every song the Beatles wrote from listening to them play over and over again. Now, decades later, the words still flow effortlessly from my lips at the first note of one of their songs.

the stage, adjusts her microphone and begins. Now, how can I put this delicately? She is less than perfect and spectacular all at the same time! She is obviously having so much fun and she is super delightful and because of these things she is charming her audience despite, and perhaps even because of, her "mistakes".

Goodbye harmonica, hello ukulele!

Soon afterwards I find my way to a local music store and stare at scads of ukuleles. I am not convinced that I will do well with this challenge because those deep-seated memories of past musical failures keep creeping into my psyche. (Oh no, I just remembered that I sucked at the brief stint of piano I tried as a teen too.)

Then I see her, a sweet little red number, a soprano apparently and conveniently the least expensive model. I hand over my fifty bucks (rather apropos, don't you think?) and we are off. From the moment I hold her in my lap, I am in love. She fits perfectly, in a way that the big bulky guitar never did. Her curves match my curves, her size matches my size and her personality matches my personality. Short, sassy, fun! I call her Ruby and who would have known we'd become best buds.

The excitement I have after purchasing this little red piece of heaven shocks even me. I had watched Lana enjoy her instrument and I had watched the crowd watch Lana enjoy her instrument. Now I just need to figure out how to make this little girl sing. I already love her so I *have* to make her sing. I can't let her down.

First stop, download a tuner from The App Store. Check. √
Next, print off a chord sheet from Google. Check. √
Then, look up some beginner, three-chord songs on YouTube. Check √
Finally, wait until everyone is out of the house and practice, practice, practice! √

The first song I learn is "Leaving on a Jet Plane" by John Denver. It feels sooooo good! I am so happy, it actually sounds like a song! Practicing is not a chore, it's a pleasure. Well I can't speak for my family, but it is a pleasure for me at least.

When you are looking for someone to appreciate what you do, many of us are lucky enough to have a mother who is our greatest fan, no matter what. So I take Ruby on the road and we go to visit Mom, who at ninety is about as sweet as a mom can be.

And guess what? She falls in love with Ruby too!

When I'm not on the road, Ruby and I visit her most every day. The first thing she says upon my arrival is, "Did you bring Ruby?"

Before long she starts to have requests–"Imagine," "Octopus' Garden," "Top of the World," "The Roller Skating Song." I've gotta tell you, when your 90-year-old mom is singing along, it's about the sweetest thing in the world. Plus, being the great mom that she is, she complimented me endlessly. My favourite line of hers is, "I can't believe I borned you." She tells me daily what a great voice I have and how incredibly talented I am. This does a lot for my self-confidence. I try not to let the fact that she is pretty much deaf take away from the flattering remarks. No one loves me like my mom does.

One day, while I am speaking at an event and talking about exploring your passions and using those as stress-release activities, I tell the audience about Ruby. Right away someone challenges me to play in public. "Ha! I don't think so!" Then one lady says, "I work at a daycare. The kids would love to sing along with a little red ukulele and they are the best audience. Mistakes won't matter at all."

And so it is decided, I will have my first public performance! My friend introduces me to the most perfect tune, the song "Lava". It's a Hawaiian story about two volcanoes and it ends with "I lava you". Perfect.

Can you picture this beautiful experience? Twenty itty, bitty, curious preschool faces of every skin shade you can imagine, sitting in a circle on the floor with all eyes on Ruby. I am nervous even in front of this friendly little audience but they don't care. They listen, clap and sing along. I pass Ruby around the circle and they make her sing. It is a very special afternoon.

Ruby becomes my stress release, my joy, my active meditation, my escape, my fun and a new way to connect and interact with others.

Ruby had unlocked the door to the world of music, a world into which I was not previously allowed. I could hardly wait for someone to ask me if I played an instrument because for the first time in my life, I could say, "Yes. Yes I do."

Sometimes it's great being wrong. After decades of thinking I could never be a musician, I am so happy to say I am. As an added bonus, I've come to notice that no one ever asks if you are a "good" musician.

Thank you Ukulele Lady for giving me permission to not be perfect, for inspiring me to play, and for showing, not telling, me what joy and passion look like.

If there was a fire in my house, I would go in to rescue Ruby, my little red love!

More about Ruby later.

In my previous life in the healthcare field, when I was providing nursing care in people's homes, I met this frail, little old man whose body was all knotted up with arthritis. I noticed that he had a piano in his apartment and asked him if he would play me a song. He obligingly hobbled his humped body to the bench and sat himself down in front of the keys. Then something magical happened. His bent-over body sat up completely straight! His gnarled up fingers straightened out and he began to play music that brought a tear to my eye. When he was finished, his body immediately curled back up to its previous state. If I hadn't seen it with my own eyes, I wouldn't have believed it. This was the first time I remember seeing passion in action and the power it has.

Try 16

retro-walking

IN WHAT WOULD probably be among the top five oddest escapades in that experiential year, I decide to explore the practice of… wait for it… backwards locomotion! Retro walking or plain old walking backwards (which doesn't sound nearly as cool, according to me) is said to both reduce the boredom of conventional walking and provide a more intense and comprehensive workout than walking forward. Because your heart rate tends to be higher than when you walk "normally" at the same pace, some research suggests that we receive increased cardiovascular and calorie-burning benefits. Plus, according to Healthline, retro walking has been found to:

- Increase strength in lesser-used leg muscles.
- Help rehabilitate knee injuries
- Improve walking technique and form
- Boost energy levels
- Help with balance
- Strengthen bones and muscles

And so, with some safety precautions in place–helmet, elbow pads and goggles (I'm kidding), I begin. The Hub walking forward actually provides my much needed eyes in the front of my head so I can retro walk at the beach, on the street, over here, over there, I can retro walk anywhere! Cue Dr. Seuss, please.

While I did expect it would be a little less boring than conventional walking, what I didn't expect was the unusual analogy for life that speaks to me. When walking forward we see where we are headed, like our lives, and we watch our future unfold before us.

What I notice when walking backward is that along with working some new muscles, I see my life in a different way. Instead of seeing my future appear in front of me, I see my past in front of me (or would that be behind me?). Either way, I see my past slipping away. It feels like an analogy for aging. The buildings and people that pass me are fading away, getting smaller, more distant. Events that have happened, people that I have met, melt into the background as they get further and further away.

It makes me think of moments in our lives that seem so huge, like graduation or our wedding day. With each step (or day) these events get further and further away and often seem less significant. Maybe it's the same thing with troubles too. They seem so huge and insurmountable at the time, but they too get smaller and smaller when looking back at them. Asking ourselves how important this current issue is going to be in a decade, a year or even a month can help us put our current "big thing" into perspective.

We often get stuck and overwhelmed by looking ahead to see how far we have to go to reach a goal, a milestone or any perceived success. Maybe once in a while we should turn around and notice how far we've already come so that we can celebrate and appreciate that which has helped us get to where we are now.

So retro walking is not a full-time thing, but every once in a while, I turn around and practice seeing life from a different perspective. If you see me, wave hello–or goodbye.

Try 17

the three second kiss

Sometimes I enjoy Try's that involve other people and sometimes I like not telling them what I'm about to do. It's sort of like a secret social experiment and typical victim, er, the benefactor, is The Hub. Such was the case with this particular Try, when I decide I want to Kaizen our relationship up a notch. I quietly observe things around the house for awhile, looking for the perfect opportunity for slyly insert a relationship hack.

Then I hear it–the sound of The Hub coming home from work. The sound of the dogs scampering to the door to greet him with enthusiasm. The sound of him playing with them. Then the sound of him calling out to me, "Hey," and my typical reply from elsewhere in the house, "Hey,"

That's when I know I have the perfect Try to try! What if when he comes home I am at least as excited as the dogs are to see him? What if I get up from my office chair or stop whatever I'm doing in the kitchen and actually walk to the door and greet him like I am happy that he is home (because I usually am!)? What if? My curiosity is going strong on this one!

This is where the *cue* comes in. A cue is a habit that is already ingrained in your psyche, something that you don't even have to think about. A cue is something that comes easily and effortlessly to you, a cue is a *trigger* to remind you to do something else. In this case, the chosen Kaizen. Without saying a word, I start implementing my experiment with the door as my cue. Whether he is coming in or out, when I hear that door it is my trigger to move. I can't wait to try this out!

The next day, as I hear the door open, the dogs move and their friendly scuffle as The Hub plays with them, I hear him say "Hey" to me and I am just about to say "Hey" back (how quickly we forget our new promises), when I suddenly remember and peel myself away from my very important computer work. I dash to the door like I am about to miss something. I embrace him with all the excitement I can muster and tell him I'm so happy he is home.

He is very quiet. He looks at me funny. Then he asks if the car is okay. He asks if there is something I want to tell him.

"Nope, it's all good, I'm just happy to see you!" I reply, and leaving him standing in his own bewilderment, back I go to my office with a smile on my face.

Later, when he is heading out, he shouts, "I'm leaving," from the door. I am just about to shout "Bye!" when I remember again. "Wait!" I yell, as I leave the kitchen and barrel on to the door to catch him before he leaves. I mean, what if I never see him again? What if this is our last goodbye? I want it to be nice; I want him to know I actually care that he's leaving.

I give him a nice hug and perfect three second kiss, longer than a peck - but not enough to get anything started (It's the perfect amount of time, I've tested it out!). He looks at me with the same odd look on his face as he heads out the door.

This continues day after day after day after day until finally one day something amazing happens. I am just about to leave the house and he is sitting in his favourite spot on the couch watching sports. I say, "Bye," and he says… "Wait."

With a magnetic-like draw and like a movie going into slow motion, he rises up from the couch and comes to the door to say goodbye to me like he actually cares I am leaving. Gasp!

To this day our comings and goings are acknowledged with this simple act that I learned from our dogs. I'm pretty sure if I were to have said to him, "You know you really should get up and greet me when I come or go from this house," it would not have been very well received. This Try worked so well that The Hub even said, "When you greet me at the door with love in your eyes, it's the best part of my day."

Awe! How do you like that Try Angle?

Try 18

hey sugar, sugar

I WOKE UP on a wintery morning with a thought in my head and a new challenge ready to burst out. It wasn't a fun, exciting challenge like some of the others, but it was one that I knew I needed to do. I was going to try fifty days without sugar. Just the thought of it gave me withdrawal systems. You see, I am a sugar junkie. In fact, a junk food junkie I'd say. Growing up with overweight parents, an abundance of food and a mom who was an amazing cook started me on my journey to unhealthy eating habits. Then as an adult I charged full-speed ahead, all on my own, to continue and unfortunately pass down (sorry, kids) the tradition.

I felt like I had to do this challenge because it seemed like I exhibited a decent amount of control in other areas of my life–but this one always seemed to elude me. Sugar was winning and it was really getting annoying.

I read a quote that resonated with me, "You can't out-train a lousy diet." I think that's what I was trying to do. I thought that since I exercised I could eat whatever I wanted. Well, of course I could, but everything comes at a cost–in this case mental clarity, weight, health, and loss of control?

Armed with Barry Friedman's book, *I Love Me More than Sugar*–I am not excited but I'm ready! Fifty days, no sugar–ready, set, go! Wait, silly me! Christmas holidays, my favourite convention, and New Year's fall within those fifty days. Bummer! Hmmm, maybe I will make a few amendments. Hey, it's my project. Don't judge me.

I give myself permission to take five days of my choosing off within those fifty days. If I slip and have some sugar on undesignated days, I will add two days to my challenge as punishment. This proves to be a great strategy because every time I pick up a sugary treat, I ask myself, "Is this worth adding two days to the Try?" Usually the answer is, "No" and I pass it up; occasionally I answer, "Yes!" and then I consciously enjoy every mouthful. For example, at this really lovely B & B in Indiana, Sharon, the mom-like owner, makes fudge just for me and I sit in front of the fireplace, scraping the sides of the bowl with a wooden spoon. Yep, this is special!

This is a far cry from the mindless eating I used to do. When I say no to a sugary treat, or choose fruit over dessert, I feel proud of myself. I can say no to a sweet treat and it doesn't kill me!

I am slowly winning this war over my sugar addiction. I am so happy with myself. It is the end of February and I am finally "finished" this challenge. But I'm worried that without the "carrot" of this challenge in front of my nose, it will be easy to slip back into my old sugar-addicted ways.

Without fail, when I ask the server for a fruit dessert at a fancy event or a convention, the most lovely (and huge) fruit platter would appear. Other people at the table always ask, '"How did you get that?" The answer is always, "I simply ask." Those fancy desserts generally look better than they taste anyway. At least, that's what I tell myself!

Instead, the most amazing thing happens. I don't crave the sugar anymore. I still love looking at it, smelling it, and appreciating it but I don't *need* it anymore. I can walk into every bakery that I pass and talk about what I would order and then I walk out. I can pass up the usual cookies, cakes and pastries without torture. The Hub also accidentally joined my on this journey and when we decided to indulge, we would both moan about how yucky our tummies felt.

The biggest win here was not in completing the fifty days without sugar, it was in choosing to be purposeful, deliberate and intentional every time I was faced with a sugar choice.

Full disclosure–this remains a daily struggle for me; many days I lose the battle, but every day is a new day for an opportunity to choose well!

$$\mathcal{T}ry \; 19$$

cuff love

Maybe you saw us walking with our dogs? Maybe you saw us in the grocery store? Maybe you didn't even notice us or maybe you noticed something was a little off but didn't know what to say.

We were the couple wearing handcuffs.

Say what? You read correctly, handcuffs. The Hub and I handcuffed ourselves together for twenty-four hours. Yes, on purpose!

I can't even remember how the conversation about doing it got started, but you know how one thing leads to another. The most frequent question people asked when they heard about this try was, "Why? Why on earth would you want to do that?"

Well, we had a lot of reasons actually, but mostly we just wanted to see *if* we could do it, how we could do it, and what would happen if we did (or didn't) make it twenty-four hours. Additionally, I wondered what the social reaction would be and hoped to discover some insights into what feelings would be uncovered.

After trying to imagine every possible scenario that would happen within a twenty-four hour period–how would we dress, sleep and even go to the bathroom, we felt confident that we could do this and were ready to start. The only thing missing was the handcuffs.

As luck would have it, our first born is a police officer. Can you think of a worse person from whom to borrow handcuffs? Ah well, here it goes… "Hey Bud," I text, "can we borrow a set of handcuffs?"

His reply comes back almost immediately, "When do you need them?" Note that his reply is not what do you need them for, simply when. Within the week he pops over with the handcuffs in tow and

WASHROOMS

gives us a crash course on how to put them on and, more importantly, take them off.

I can't help but ask him, "Bud, when you got the text about us
wanting to borrow the handcuffs, did you not wonder *why* we wanted them?" To which he replied, "First of all, it's you, so no I didn't
wonder. Second of all, in policing, if you don't want know the answer,
you don't ask the question."

Good point... and so that's how we find ourselves clinked
together with an official set of Smith and Wesson handcuffs.

It is a weekend so we don't have any "real" work to deal with, but
together we do the mundane things that couples do such as make
the bed, make meals, make... chocolate. We go for walks, we shop,
we clean the pool and watch a show. We entertain and visit relatives.
I'm certain if you ask our company and relatives, we are even more
entertaining than usual!

The funny thing is that while we are out in public not a single
person asks us about the handcuffs. Not one! Would you have?

More importantly than garnering attention for our escapades is
what we learned from doing this Try. It is immeasurable.

We learned that we are pretty darned compatible–good thing

after thirty-plus years of being together! We had to communicate better, compromise more, cooperate fully and plug our noses on occasion! We had to take turns, work together, practice patience and be respectful. Did I mention be patient?

We had to go without privacy, sleep on the "wrong" side of the bed and get up when we weren't ready. Think about it–we literally couldn't even remove our shirts.

Things that were simple instantly became complicated. Tasks that we didn't think twice about suddenly involved the other person. Immediately, pretty much every decision we made involving movement, the other person had a vested interest in.

Again the question that bubbles to the surface is why? Why put yourself through the stress of an experiment like this?

The answer isn't really that hard because every time we push, pull and challenge ourselves, every time we do something outside the norm, every time we do something that shakes up what we know, we emerge a tiny bit different, a tiny bit better than we were before.

Whether you use Smith and Wessons, zip ties or a scarf, I would highly recommend trying this or something similar with your special person.

You might say no way, we could never do that, but I ask you to think conceptually here. Literally, yes, of course, you could tie yourselves together for twenty-four hours like we did. Or you could do it for eight or four or two hours. Or you do for longer periods with breaks for fifteen minutes every four hours or… this is the beautiful thing about this or any idea–it's your experiment, it's your life, you can try! You can challenge yourself in any way you'd like. You can make up the rules, change the rules or throw out the rules!

Whatever you do, you may just come out loving each other more, with some fresh insight or understanding or with some new tools to help your relationship grow. If you are lucky, you will have fun and enjoy being close, and when someone says "What's new?" well, you can decide for yourself whether or not to tell. But if you tell, you can be sure everyone will lean in to listen!

Try 20

go veggie

HAVE YOU ever attended a webinar? I do try to catch some now and again. Usually I'm doing thirteen other things at the same time (which is why I don't like to give webinars–I know what you are doing while I am presenting!).

This one caught my attention. They are vegans. No meat. No dairy products. No eggs. I jump on this webinar that some colleagues of mine are hosting called *Healthy and Happy*–because those are two of my favourite words. "They" are power women Gina Carr and Karen Jacobson (Karen happens to be the voice of Siri Australia who tells me where to go all the time.) and while I expected to learn some things about living healthier during the webinar, what I didn't expect was to be given a challenge that would profoundly affect my life for what may be ever.

The challenge was to go vegan for thirty days. Gulp.

I listened, I thought, I considered. Then I declined and sought to negotiate. It was my year and I had reserved the right to negotiate.

Instead of thirty days a vegan, how about fifty days a vegetarian?

Fifty days a vegetarian sounded reasonable, and as goals should be—it was a bit of a stretch but doable.

Even as a child I was attracted to vegetarianism. When I was parenting small children I thought about it here and there, but I just didn't have the energy to be creative enough to figure it out. I guess I didn't want it badly enough.

Does that sound *Jeopardy*-like to you? I'll take Vegetarian for fifty, Alex.

But now the time was right and for fifty days I intend to be a vegetarian.

Day 1 is easy, on Day 2, I forget and with a gasp realize I have just polished off a croissant with meat inside, oops. And so I began anew…

Day 1, easy. Day 2, easy. Day 3–"Wow, that looks good!" And that's when I realize that I am not going to be practicing vegetarianism.

I learn a new and lesser known word–pescatarian, which is a vegetarian who eats fish and seafood. I decide to try this out. I think that if I had to capture my own food, the chances of me eating a cow, pig or chicken is slim to none, but the chances of me catching my food in the water is high. That becomes my criteria.

Three weeks into my challenge our summer holiday finds us making our way through Italy–otherwise known as the button-popping country of Eataly. Since Italian is my heritage, I know that of everything I will miss during my vegetarian challenge–like my favourite burger joint, the perfectly cooked steak and even that rare but extremely enjoyed European wiener with the hard skin–that far and away the hardest thing for me to give up will be what I had grown up with, Italian cured meats. That will be the absolute hardest meat to turn away from. It feel like not indulging while on this once in a lifetime trip would be, well, almost sacrilegious. I am perfectly prepared to take a break from my vegetarianism during this holiday and commit to resuming upon my arrival back home–I will add an extra couple of weeks on the back end of the challenge.

But something surprising happens when we get to Italy. Even though every shop is full of sandwiches bursting with every variety of favourite meats from my childhood, even though The Hub said the meatballs tasted just like my mom's and even though the lasagna was a toppling tower filled with meat sauce, I just don't want to eat them.

I am kind of excited. I think that I am becoming a pescatarian for real–like, permanently. It is something that, for over forty years, has been calling to me and I so pleased that I am finally able to answer the call.

We start watching documentaries on vegetarianism and "they" say that even cutting back, say incorporating a Meatless Monday once a week, is helpful and contributes to a more conscious eating style.

Now I actually get excited about new recipes, unique vegetables, trying creative things in the kitchen, and making choices that I am proud of. It all feels good. I don't feel like I'm missing out.

It's funny, when my kids were growing up, if a smoke detector went off, someone would say, "Mom's cooking!" (Read "Don't let the Grilled Cheese Win" in my first book, *When Enlightening Strikes*, for more on this topic).

After trying dozens of new recipes, both vegetarian and vegan, I have become quite a kick-ass cook, if I do say so myself!

Maybe it's not that I couldn't cook. Maybe it's just that I couldn't (shouldn't) cook meat!

Try 21

excuse me, I burpeed

I DECIDED to do a thirty-day burpee fitness challenge. If you don't know what a burpee is, I have to wonder how you got through gym class? Anyway, a burpee is a wicked cardio movement that integrates a push up, a squat and a jump in rapid succession–you can just call it torture for short.

For the thirty-day challenge, I decided that every day for a month I would do burpees first thing in the morning. I would start with one and each day I would increase it by one. How hard could this be?

Hard.

For the first few days it is easy. Day 1, Day 2, Day 3, no prob. But around Day 10, I start breathing heavily and it isn't the good kind of breathing heavy.

By Day 25, I think I am going to die, but then I remember what I'd learned in my first challenge... usually when you think you are going to die, you aren't, except for that one time when you actually do.

Although this may not appear to be the most exciting challenge, the lesson acquired here was of mammoth proportions. If I would have started by trying to do thirty burpees, I would have stopped by Day 2, but by employing *The Try Angle* I was able to keep it going.

Don't ask "If", ask "How". That is, don't ask if you can use the information, ask how you can use the information. How can you combine this idea with another? How can you move the information into another area of your life? How can... ? You get the idea.

With Kaizen in my back pocket I was able to ask myself, "How can I use the concept of small, continuous improvement in my own life?" If I had proceeded too slowly with my burpee challenge, I would have been bored, not seen progress and likely would have quit–same goes if it was too big of a goal for me.

As great as Kaizen is, it in itself is not always enough; at least it isn't for me. Too often we listen to a speaker, read a book or capture a great idea from somewhere and declare, "Yes! I'm going to do that!" Then we walk to the bottom of the stairs and we forget what we went down there for–do you know what I mean? We move on to the next thing and poof, we totally forget what improvement we were going to make.

K + C - Kaizen (K), the small improvement, for me it was daily burpees. The Cue (C) was first thing in the morning. Do not pass go, do not collect $200, do not stop at the bathroom… wait… for the burpees you'd better stop at the bathroom! The point is that if I'd have said I would do my burpees "sometime" during the day, I could pretty much guarantee you that "sometime" would never have come. Because I tied the Kaizen in with the Cue, success was mine!

This is not a big thing, it's a little thing, I get that. However, I truly believe that one day we are all going to realize that the little things *are* the big things. That it is all these little things that add up to create health, happiness, positivity, great relationships, vitality and all sorts of good stuff that we can't get enough of! .

Back to the burpees–one point.

Speaking of points. Were we speaking of points? No, but we were talking about small things and small things make me think of points. I like to give myself points—it's the game lover in me. I give myself a point when I do something that leans me in closer to being healthier, happier, kinder, friendlier—all that good stuff. Everything is worth a point. One point. Big things, small things, medium things—everything is worth one point. I greet The Hub at the door, one point; I buy him a car, one point. I hold the door open for a stranger, one point, I return a wallet full of hundred dollar bills, still one point.

Try 22

art or bust

MY FRIEND is an artist of epic proportions. Cheryl-Ann Webster is the creator of the *Beautiful Women Project*–an amazing endeavour she started to help women feel, well–feel beautiful!

When Cheryl-Ann found out about my 50/50 List she immediately challenged me with an art project.

Now I hardly know one end of a paintbrush from the other and I'm pretty sure as a kid my art never even made it onto the fridge (feel my pain). However, the thing with a project like the 50/50 List is that if you ask for challenges, you kind of have to be prepared to do them, at least some variation of them anyway.

And so it begins, even though we are three provinces apart, a commitment from us both to take an art journey to places yet unknown.

The first order of the day is to get tools of the trade. Cheryl-Ann writes me a list, most of which I can't understand. It will be the first time in my life I enter an art supply store and it is like I am in a foreign foods emporium–I have no idea what things even are. Feeling like a parent shopping for school supplies for the first time, I hand my list to the clerk, step back and give her full reign to fill my basket.

One hundred and fifty dollars later (which I am happy to invest, btw), I have bags of goodies–some excite me, some scare me, and some I don't even know what to do with.

Explore, express and evolve. That is the theme my artist/coach shares with me during our first session.

We start with the watercolour pencils. I unwrap the cellophane from the tin to reveal twelve perfectly perfect coloured pencils. They are beautiful! So beautiful in fact that I don't want to use them. Remember opening a new box of crayons? It is like that–minus the smell.

She gives me some guidelines on how to use and care for the pencils and brushes and then we begin with a self-portrait.

Self-portrait!! What the… ?? That scares the heck out of me!

Cheryl-Ann helps me to see a new side of self-portraits and I quickly understand that this is not about making a perfect piece of art. This is about finding what is on the inside of me and bringing it out. Ohhhhh. What a totally different experience!

She asks me to hold the coloured pencils in my non-dominant hand. My dominant hand all but says–Hey, that's my job!" She then tells me to hold the pencil in a different way than I usually do–and my fingers scream, "Wrong!"

In everything we do, she challenges me to break the rules, to not do the logical thing. Everything we do causes me to feel and think differently.

The lovely pencils start to get used. They have been dipped in water and become a bit messy. I reconcile my sadness when the paper, blank just moments before, starts coming to life. I am still pretty sure it isn't going to hang on the fridge, but it is… well, interesting! Using the brushes on the pencil strokes turns the colors into yet another expression.

I am having a great time and soon our 90 minute session is almost up. She asks me to open up the tin of lead pencils.

And that's when things get tough.

I hold the new tin in my hands, unable to unwrap the cellophane. She asks me what is wrong and I say I think we should save them for the next session. Then the artist/coach starts digging. She starts asking those darned, thought-provoking questions that I am supposed to ask clients, not the other way around.

As it turns out, this art lesson literally brings me to tears. It feels too decadent to open both tins on the same day. It felt like "too much"–like I didn't need, or in fact, deserve to have both tins opened.

Gently, but with conviction, Cheryl-Ann says she knows that frugality has worked well for me in the past; it helped me get what I need. She says that while there is still a place for it in my life, there is also a room for abundance. Abundance and frugality can work together.

Then from the other side of the computer screen she takes one of her shiny new pencils and breaks it in half. I just gasp. It's okay. Everything's okay. We can use things when they are perfect and we can use things when they are broken. We can be both frugal and abundant.

The whole experience is so emotional it actually gives me goosebumps. Art, I was learning, is about so much more than the finished product.

Our creativity-coaching continues monthly exploring all sorts of wild media for self-expression and again I find myself in a world that was previously elusive and unknown to me. The world of art had opened its doors and welcomed little ol' me inside.

I have fun in that art world. I start packing my brushes and watercolour pencils (which, after trying many different media, seem to be my favourite). and I start making cards for people. I begin using art as my recharge, reset, down time–my me time.

But this one time, for this one very special project… I need The Hub. We are creating a bust cast.

Cheryl-Ann has done this hundreds of times, The Hub and I have never done it before. She warns us that it will be messy. We are ready!

Picture the basement covered in plastic. I am the model standing motionless and topless in front of my beloved. This is no time for funny business; this is serious stuff here. He must work quickly, efficiently and thoroughly!

My beloved plasters me from the neck down and the waist up with Vaseline. Lots of Vaseline. A thick layer. Everywhere—all the creases, caverns and protrusions (yes, belly buttons and nipples). This stage is very important so that we can get the cast off easily. Slather it on!

Next, strips of casting material, dipped in tepid water, are laid this way and that way across my torso. The sensations are unlike anything I have experienced before—the oiliness of the Vaseline, the coolness of the water, the mushiness of the plaster, and the pressure of the hands smoothing, pinching and tucking things into place. As the last layers go on, I can start to feel the hardened part of the cast coming away from my body. The whole experience is very odd!

My beloved takes his role very seriously, this is not a sexy time— he is in work mode! About an hour later, the cast falls easily off my torso thanks to the copious amounts of Vaseline in which I'm covered. Now the cast must dry for a few days before the actual project of painting the bust begins.

All is well until Gina discovers the cast drying in our basement, is horrified and very likely scarred for life. (We thought we'd hid it pretty well–apparently not.) Despite this trauma she feels compelled to make a video about it to share with her online world.

"You can't make this stuff up," she begins. She interviews me, The Hub and The Bust, of course, and it is actually hilarious. The Hub shows off his creation to the online world and she prods him, "Is this how you keep your marriage spicy?" "It's one of the ways," he replies with a smirk. Shoot me now.

The cast is now a fully camouflaged piece of "art" that hangs on our bedroom wall and you really have to look closely to be able to tell what it is. When you come to visit, maybe I'll show you.

Then again, maybe not. It may scar you for life, too.

Try 23

flag, star and thrown

WHAT KIND OF YOGA? Afro–as in African? No Acro–as in acrobatic!

Acrobatic and I would only ever be put in the same sentence if it were to be something like... I am going to *watch* an acrobat, or perhaps... I enjoyed the acrobat. Or even... I wasn't born to be an acrobat.

Until the challenge to try Acro-Yoga, which is a mix of partner acrobatics, Thai massage and yoga, I had never heard of it. The Hub and I had tried couple's yoga before–a beautiful, gentle, assisted stretching type of yoga practice and we liked that. We had tried Thai massage, which is basically using your body parts to massage your partner's body parts (Doesn't that sound like fun!) and we thought it was fantastic. So it was just this wee part about the acrobatics that had us a little concerned.

Nonetheless, armed with yoga mats and good faith, we enter the warm, hardwood floored studio with perhaps just a bit of trepidation. We are definitely not yogis and we are full on at least twenty years older than most everyone in the room. We look at each other, shrug our shoulders and roll out our mats. I silently thank The Hub for joining me, yet again, on this challenge that requires two. As we wait for the class to begin, we copy the young yogis and do a warm-up stretch and try not to stand out too much.

It's hard to describe Acro-Yoga, but I'll try. Basically, one person is the "base", the support person, and the other is the "flyer", the one who is balancing. Despite the fact that it is a beginner's class, they waste no time getting us "flying" each other in the air, supporting each other's body weight and coaxing us into positions we could never have dreamed.

Some of the moves, with names such as Flag, Star, Thrown, Reverse Bird and Candle, are used to communicate what move is to be done next. Some require "spotters" so we have to be in groups of three.

This means touching, trusting and sometimes falling on top of scantily clad and often sweaty strangers. "Umm, sorry," was pretty much all I can say as I land awkwardly on top of a young gentleman and scramble to get up as quickly as possible.

During this all new-to-us hour of Acro-Yoga, we learn many new things. We have to trust ourselves, each other and strangers. We have to touch each other and strangers, and we have to have faith that the instructors aren't going to let us kill ourselves!

By the end of our first class we had stretched, flown, tumbled, sweated, connected, laughed, and high-fived!

On the ride home we both declared we had fun, held our own with those youngins and we begin planning when we will go again. Yep, we are hooked!

We start capturing moves from Pinterest and YouTube and, not only do we do Acro at the classes, we do it at our home, in the park, and at the beach. While we aren't especially good, we are good enough to impress people with some cool moves. We start sharing some moves with friends and recruiting others to come to class. It is a bit addicting!

The best line came from my middle-est Kara (who has since joined the Acro cult following). We are in the basement practicing and falling all over the place. She is getting ready to go out and waiting for her friends to arrive. She comes over and stands towering over our tumbled down bodies, motions toward us and says, "This needs to be done before my friends get here." Gotcha, and a new Note-to-Self: no Acro-Yoga when the kids' friends are over.

What The Hub and I love most about Acro is that sometimes we'd see a move that we were sure we couldn't do, then we'd discover that, with an open mind, a trusted partner, practice, patience, failure and, of course, *The Try Angle*, we'd have success. When it finally comes together it feels so great! We feel like we've accomplished something, had fun and grown closer in the process. There are times though when we cannot get the pose, or we can only get the pose with assistance, and we learn that that's okay too.

Maybe that's why I like Acro-Yoga, because it's a lot like life—fun, challenging and rewarding.

Try 24

lights, camera, action

MY SPEAKER FRIEND Martin is a bright light in the world of online video. When we shared the stage at a conference in Arizona he challenged me to use video to spread my message of positive living.

I'm sure I let out an audible sigh as I let the challenge sink in. The effort it would take, not the content so much as the… well the "me."

You know women and video–hair, makeup, pressure to look a certain way. Ick. I'm a low maintenance gal and makeup and I, let's just say we don't get along all that well. Despite that fact that my daughter Gina is a talented freelance makeup artist, for me it's a chore, and the truth is that most of the makeup I own is older than she is.

And then there's my hair. I've had this hair for 50 years and I still don't know what to do with it.

With all that in the back of my mind, it took me from February, when the challenge was issued, until September to suck up the courage, to get out of my own way and to actually start.

On September 1st, Facebook Live and I become friends. With no script, no hair done and no makeup on (gasp) I start filming with the purpose not so much to educate, entertain or inspire, but to push myself into the uncomfortable.

The videos, ranging in length from about three to twenty minutes, basically are… "This is me and this is what I'm doing today. This is where I am today. This is a tip or a thought for the day… blah, blah, blah."

Producing these videos is quite torturous at first and I certainly don't want to watch them. But as the weeks pass I can tell I am getting, if not comfortable, at least less *un*comfortable with doing them. The very odd time, it is even... fun!

The only way I can continue is by not putting too much thought into what I am doing, by being intentionally ignorant (I don't want to know what my audience thinks about them), and by not thinking about what other professionals are doing with their videos because they would obviously be better. I know that if I do think too much I will stop.

I realize that I do this "not thinking" thing a lot; it is both a blessing and a curse. I find if I let myself think about failure, judgement, or even potential negative consequences, I miss so many opportunities. So I just do, as with the videos, right or wrong. I just do them for thirty days in a row. One with no sound, one with the camera facing the wrong way, one with the lens blocked, one where I cry, and on and on.

As I reflect back on the videos I made–in the radio station, in the TV studio, in my backyard, after a conference, in the stadium, after a run, after a meeting, during a meeting, interviewing others, impromptu and imperfect–they were... fine. They were good enough. I wasn't forcing people to watch them because after all, people could choose.

By the end of September, I was more comfortable, I felt less self-conscious and I think I got better at it too.

For the most part the comments were good, the views between five hundred and a thousand. They were nowhere near Martin's number but I'm grateful for his challenge and my Facebook peeps for spending their valuable time with me.

I didn't continue with the daily videos, but I do them whenever the spirit moves me. I am vigilant for something interesting in my travels, in my day, or in my world worthy of sharing, of interest, inspiration or education to my online world. Feel free to find me online, I'll be your friend!

We are often our own biggest obstacle. With *The Try Angle*, we can all try to get out of our own way a little more often.

Try 25

hair today, gone tomorrow

I LOVE having my personal and business world associated with doing good. Each day I realize how blessed I am. When I can do good for others by giving blood or collecting warm clothes, it is a way of saying thanks to the universe, a wee bit of payback.

Almost every month I lead some sort of fundraiser for one cause or another, usually switching between local and global not-for-profits. We do 50/50 draws (and it always warms my heart when the winners give their portion back to the charity). Our family does donations instead of gifts.

I decided I wanted to do something really big, to raise a lot of money and I knew exactly how to do it! I just wasn't sure if I wanted to do it. The Hub was very sure he didn't want me to do it.

I just knew if I shaved off my long brown hair for The Children's Hospital in our city, people would get out their credit cards to support the mission. I just knew it. My sister thought people would donate without me shaving my head. My friend said she would pay me not to shave my head. But I just knew that *this* was the ticket to the big fundraiser I had wanted to do as a part of my 50/50 challenge.

"Why are you doing this?" my youngest asked. She was very vocal about her displeasure at my decision to lop off all 12 inches of my hair. "It's a fundraiser." I told her. "That's not the only reason, why are you really doing it?" she prodded.

Ahhh, most of us have that one kid who calls us out, who challenges and provokes us. Wouldn't life be boring without those kids? As I reflected, I realized that she was 100% correct. There was a reason beyond raising funds and awareness, a reason perhaps even more important to me than raising funds. The problem was… I didn't know yet exactly what that reason was.

I was presenting to healthcare professionals in the United States recently and after I was done I popped into the hospital gift shop to take a look-see. I held a sweater in front of me trying the colour on for size. "That colour looks so nice with your hair," the senior behind the counter said.

"Oh, that doesn't matter, it will all be gone soon," I said without skipping a beat. I didn't think anything of what I had said. I knew what I was talking about. I knew that I would be shaving my head soon, not because I had to, but because I was choosing to. I knew, but, of course, she didn't. She immediately thought I was sick. I could tell that's what she thought because right away she started treating me noticeably differently, in that "oh poor dear" sort of way. Interesting.

I had been thinking about this for over a year. It took that long for me to get The Hub to agree. I can't explain it exactly. I felt like I had to do it. It's not about the courage to do the shave, but rather it's about the vulnerability for me to have a shaved head. To not have hair to hide behind and to see, really see, myself. I am not young, nor model material. To see my high forehead, my Italian nose, my non-aerodynamic ears, my neck, exposed. All. Of. Me. I was scared and I knew I had to do it. I couldn't Kaizen my way out of this one. I didn't know what would happen but I knew I would emerge on the other side of this experience different in some way.

As the evening of the event approaches, I am increasingly more frightened. I will have my head shaved on stage in front of hundreds of people. "How will I react? Will it be freeing? Will I laugh? Will I cry? Will I be filled with regret? How will The Hub react to me? Will it affect my career? Will I be able to be myself on stage and finish the show with confidence?" I have no idea what will transpire. It's just hair and thankfully for me it's a renewable resource. It's just hair. It's just hair. At least that's what I keep telling myself as the date loomed.

It is going to happen at the November momondays, the show I

produce nine times a year. It's an entertaining, happy, positive place for speakers to share stories, for audience members to garner inspiration and motivation, and there is always a little audience interaction.

The first task is to fill up the house. The more people there, the more money we can raise.

- Three hundred and fifty people. Check √

- Now, find a sponsor to match the donations. Check √

- Plan a kick-ass show with local celebrities. Check √

- Get a wig sponsor so that I will have hair for my job as a professional speaker. Check √ (I really feel like I can do hair-free day-to-day but not for my job–people are hiring the person on my website and I will not look like that person anymore. This look will be distracting and I don't want the look to distract from the message. I will wear a wig for work.)

The show goes great and I feel trepidation but there is never a thought that I will back out. This head shave is definitely happening.

In between acts, just as I had planned, we have a wig-off. I am fitted with two wigs and the audience chooses their favourite. A little while later we do another two wigs and they choose again. I love getting the audience involved in the show! Just before the grand finale of the evening, the actual shave, the audience chooses which of the wigs I will be wearing to work. Can you believe it is a tie? I turn to The Hub to have him make the final call.

And now it is time, my time… shave time.

People who donate over a hundred dollars can come up on stage and literally shave a strip of my hair off. Even though I know that about a dozen people have donated this amount, only three actually want to do the deed to me.

I sit in the chair with the typical black plastic cape wrapped around me. Then I hear it, the buzz of the electric shaver. I have never heard that sound so close to my ear before.

I start to feel the emotions build inside me, but we keep it light and we joke as each person approaches, has a four-second lesson on what to do with the razor and then takes a strip off me. There is no mirror, so all that I can see is their hand full of my hair, detached from my body. Gulp.

Then over the sound system, the song I had requested, "Try" by Colbie Caillat, begins. This song is about being vulnerable, exposed, being your authentic self in front of others. It is the perfect song for this experience and when I hear the first note, my chin begins to quiver and the tears begin to well up.

The stage is empty. It is just me, the razor and Jen, the hair stylist (who would later post that this was the most inspiring and memorable experience of her entire career).

I sit still. I take big breaths. I close my eyes. I feel the razor go from back to front. I feel the hair fall alongside my face. I feel the tears fall down my cheeks. The Hub, who appears when my eyes are closed, clenches my hand reassuringly.

I hear the buzz. I hear the words of the song. I hear people shouting encouraging words. I hear silence.

I notice everything–my head getting lighter and cooler, the brush of Jen's "sweeper" brush on my face dusting off the hairs, and the cape coming off.

I hear the applause and whistles and howls. I slowly peel my eyes open, head down, and see lots of long dark hair at my feet. When I raise my gaze I see 350 supportive people on their feet, clapping, cheering and filled with emotion. I extend my arms and twirl around to show them that I'm okay, it's okay, we are all going to be okay.

I leave the stage to the heartfelt hugs of my husband, my kids and my sister. As I leave the theatre to say goodbye to the guests in the lobby as I always do, Jen slips a mirror in front of me, "You look beautiful," she says. Finally, I take my first peek at my number two buzz. It is shocking but it is still me. I'm still me.

As the guests leave, many stopping to hug, say kind words and, of course touch my head, I feel so loved. Even my friend who had offered to pay me not to do it came by. I thought about the original song Sierra Noble sang that night, "Be Who You Be." This is who I be now. I be a 51-year-old woman who shaved off a perfectly good head of hair.

My head is empty but my heart is full. Because it is such a great cause, because of generous people and because I did something bold, we raised $16,800 dollars to support sick kids. There was no Kaizen for this challenge; a trim wouldn't have made us that kind of money. This was just pure curiosity and a solid commitment. Sometimes a girl's gotta do what a girl's gotta do.

That night at home, there is another hurdle to overcome. My beautiful daughter with long golden hair, the one who thought this was the worst idea I have ever had, the one who said, "Do not do this," who left no room to wonder where she stood, and the one who would not come to watch, needed to see the results. She opened her door a crack to take a reluctant peek. I guess it's like an accident, you can't not watch. She sees me and says, "Oh my God!" and her door clicks shut.

I burst into tears. I cannot handle shoving down the emotion anymore. I go to look in the mirror and I cry some more. Then the sweetest, most supportive, most loving husband takes my hands and says, "Look at me. Look at me, looking at you. You are beautiful."

What more can a girl ask for?

I put on a hat, it's chilly without hair, and go to bed, emotionally spent.

Try 26

life after hair

THE NEXT DAY I have nothing on the calendar, no appointments, no meetings. It's just me and my head. I look in the mirror unsure of what to think. At least my head isn't full of moguls, it is smooth and nicely shaped. That is something for which I'm grateful.

I touch my head; it feels so funny and foreign. I had often asked my daughter's boyfriend if I could touch his head after he got it shaved. Is that weird? I loved how it felt all prickly. Now my head feels just like that.

Avoiding the mirrors, I have a shower. I don't even know what to do in the shower, it's like there is nothing *to* do. I'm showered and dried in a handful of minutes. Hmmm. I realize I have gained about six hours a week not having to wash, dry, style and straighten my hair—an added bonus and something else I appreciate.

The following day I have a speaking engagement with forty criminal lawyers–a tough crowd. I cannot show up bald. I better practice putting on this wig. I flip it onto my head and stare at myself. I feel even more foreign and more strange than I did being bald. The audience picked this wig for me? I take it off almost immediately and start a conversation with myself. "Can I go to this job au natural? What will the person who hired me think? What will the audience think? Will I be able to "perform" as usual? Will I be too self-conscious? What was I thinking booking an engagement so close to this challenging event? I need more time to adjust!"

I dig out my jewelry box. I think earrings will be more important now. Previously, I would put on one pair and be good for the month.

And makeup. My whole makeup department fits into the tiniest size cosmetic bag. Luckily, my daughter, who will now at least look at me, is a makeup artist. Her bathroom looks like the counter at Mac. In her own special way of saying it is going to be okay, she helps me up my makeup game. It's very complicated this makeup thing, so many brushes and powders, contours and highlights and sprays and oh my gosh–the time I will save on hair will easily be used up on face.

I sit on her toilet obediently while she dusts and puffs and strokes and blends. "You put your eyes on first so that you can clean up the fallout before you put on your face," she states matter-of-factly. Fallout? What the heck is that? Sounds like something to be wary of after a nuclear attack.

She has at least two dozen cosmetic brushes and I just nod and pretend to understand what she is talking about. I know I will absorb pretty much nothing of what she is saying but I appreciate her interest and efforts immensely.

In the end, I put on some jewelry, more makeup than usual (but less than my girl would like), leave the wig behind and show up as my new self. The meeting planner had explained to the team what I had done in advance so it will be fine. I start out feeling very self-conscious, but once I get into my groove I forget about my new look.

After spending two hours with this group and having a really meaningful time together, I ask if a few women will stay back and talk with me about my hair, or lack thereof.

Half a dozen ladies, and one gentleman who asks if he can stay, sit down with me. I ask them to be frank. I tell them about the wig and I ask them what they thought when they first saw me. Two thought I was sick, the others thought I was edgy or making a fashion statement. None thought it detracted from the message at all and they all voted for me to stay away from the wig.

That night I return the wig to my sponsor. Perhaps she can give it to someone who really needs it. I'll be okay.

Two days in, I undress for my shower. This time I stop and really look in the mirror. It's me. All of me. No hair, no makeup, no clothes.

There is so much skin. Nothing is covering my forehead, my ears, or my neck. Everything is exposed. I feel so many things.

Then I lean forward and I really look at myself. It's what I imagine I would look like if I were to be sick, except I am not. I am strong and fit and healthy. I have no bruises or scars from surgery. I do not have a disease ravaging my body. I have not been injected with drugs that kill a disease and poison a patient at the same time. My body is rejecting nothing. Why should I complain?

I think about all the women who have had to deal with all those things, plus the loss of their hair. I think about all the children who are too young to understand what they are being put through and why. I think about the parents of sick children who would trade places in an instant. I realize in that moment that all I have to deal with is no hair. Small potatoes. I am so lucky.

At that moment, I know that I'll be fine. Really, really fine. This is how I look now and I'm good. Fortunate. I knew I was blessed before, but now I know it on a deeper level. I am already so grateful for these lessons and I know there are more to come.

The next day I'm off to the airport for a job in the United States. It's not my supportive hometown audience, nor is it an audience that's been given a heads-up. It's real people with no idea what's going on. I am ready to take this head on the road–bring it on!

"Am I paranoid or are people looking at me differently? I swear people's eyes are going straight to the top of my head. It doesn't feel normal. Maybe I'm imagining things? No. Nope. I'm not. I'm definitely not." Not everyone, but many, look at my head and generally one of two things happen. They either avert their eyes or they give me the "poor dear" look. Interesting. I put on a big smile and try to look as healthy and happy as possible as I maneuver through the airports.

If I have a conversation with someone, I start out with, "I'm not sick" which is sort of a weird way to start a conversation. Upon the recommendation of a friend who had done a similar thing, I begin to change my vocabulary to, "I was involved in a fundraiser," while pointing to my head. That helped.

It's the fourth day after the head shave and I am presenting in front of a group who already knows and likes me; I'm comfortable here. They have followed my journey on Facebook and are so supportive. On this day, something wonderful happens. They tell me they have been so inspired that they are turning all of their annual "just for fun events" into a fundraising opportunities and are looking for sponsors to match donations! Now that's what I'm talking about! Inspiration, ideas,and action! This is so not about my hair–it's much, much bigger than that.

I leave their event happy and jazzed, but I miss my turn off the interstate to my hotel. My detour has me staring right at a hair salon. My gut allows the car to park in its lot. I go in and ask for a hair tattoo. What? What! What. What am I doing? The Hub and I didn't talk about this. This isn't the plan. Five minutes later the lovely Kelsey has placed a perfectly shaped heart behind my right ear. How fun is that?

If you are anything like me and you've had a baby, you may remember how modest you felt about your body before delivery and how, after the fact, you really didn't care anymore who saw what. Well, I felt that way about my hair. At first it was like, "Oh no, I could never... fill in the blank... to my hair." Now I really could care less what happens up there.

I can't decide if the heart softens my new edgy look or if it really pushes the edgy look further. You know what–I really don't care anymore.

For the first time in my life I go blond. I even try streaks of crazy colors and I'm having a blast. It's time to be who you be and for now, this is who I be. How fun is that?

Try 27

I got it all

IF YOU haven't noticed, I like to be busy, I like to have things to do. I function better at a nice steady pace. Boring and I do not do well together.

Perhaps this is why it drives me nuts when so many people complain about being soooo busy–between work, the kids activities, socializing and house things there just isn't time to… hold on there. If you are one of these people–let's chat for a moment. Most of these things on your list you signed up for, you get to do–as in they are privileges. Going to work–yep, pretty lucky to have that on your list–the alternative is not so good. Going to work means you are smart and dependable and the fact they actually make you work at work–well that's why they call it work! Next–kids' lessons, again another privilege. You can afford it and your kids are capable enough to participate in them. I could go on and on, but my two cents is that most of the things we complain about we signed up for, we actually want to do and, in fact, we would complain about being bored if we didn't have them. But what do I know?

Personally, I want to try being bored and I know I will have to be physically away from my home and office to do it. So out goes the request on Facebook looking for a place to spend twenty-four hours alone, disconnected from both people and technology. And that's how I end up in a tipi on forty acres in rural Manitoba. I am perplexed by what to pack. I know what not to pack: computer, cell phone, books–I don't want anything external coming into my time alone. I know I have to bring food and a change of clothes, but is bringing a pen and a journal "cheating"? Can I bring Ruby, my Uke? In the end, I decide as with all Try's, this Try is mine. I own it so I can make, break or change the rules. I say,"Yes," to pen and paper and to Ruby, who is no doubt thrilled to be coming along.

The closer I get to the tipi, the more surprised I am at how nervous I am getting. I'm not scared of being in the woods overnight by myself, I'm scared of being alone with just myself for company, with no distractions, no clutter, no nothing but me. Is it strange that scares me?

When the owner drops me off, she senses my apprehension, "Are you going to be okay?" she asks. "I hope so," I stutter. I mean, how bad can I be to hang out with?

Before she leaves she tells me how to pee standing up. Awesome, an extra bonus Try I wasn't expecting. Soon Tracy ATVs herself out of there and I am alone. Like really, really alone.

Something about being in the tipi feels very sacred. At twenty-four feet across and twenty feet high (that's two storeys), with a fire pit in the middle, this is not your average pup tent! Couple that with the fact that it was erected by spiritual leader and Chief of the Sioux Valley Dakota Nation Wanbdi Wakita and I barely want to leave its comforting leather walls.

They had a tipi erection party. Am I too old to think that's funny?

I force myself out to wander around in the woods a bit; the sounds I hear amidst the quiet are so beautiful–it's nature, flora and fauna, at its best. Back in the tipi I make a fire—it's so cool to watch the smoke billow out of the opening at the top of the tipi. I eat, I sleep, I pee (yes, standing up), I sleep some more. Doing nothing is really exhausting.

I sit down and noodle around with Ruby. I find a chord

progression that sounds nice and words start coming out of my mouth. Except that they are not words, they are lyrics. I am composing a song. Quickly I go get my pen and journal; I have to write this down right away before I forget. My very first song, a Try that I wasn't even trying to try, how fun!

It feels like only a few hours have passed when I hear the buzz of the ATV coming to pick me up. "Is twenty-four hours over already?" I ask incredulously. And it was. Next time sign me up for forty-eight, I kinda like my own company after all, just like my mom, who quite likes her own company!

By the way, my first song is called "I Got it All" because sitting there in that tipi in the middle of nowhere, with nobody, is where I realized that I do.

Try 28

so many try's, so little time

NOT ALL of the Try's were game changers; some just were fun and/or interesting to me. In case you want some ideas for yourself…

Post-It Notes - I left fifty Post-it notes anonymously in random and unusual places. My favourite place to leave them was on the tray tables in airplanes. I would put things like: "You are flying, isn't that amazing!" "You look fabulous!" "Today is your lucky day." "You've got the best seat in the house." "Say something complimentary to your seatmate." Sometimes I left them in public bathrooms on vending machines. It sort of felt like reverse vandalism, sneaky and fun but not bad!

The Float Spa - Granted this didn't take too much effort on my part but it was a new experience. One hour in complete and utter darkness and silence. Floating weightless in equal parts magnesium sulphate (epsom salts) and water. So dense is the mixture that you float effortlessly on top of the body temperature water. It was a strange date night indeed; The Hub and I in separate rooms and tanks. It was an interesting experience nonetheless, especially for a person who is not used to being still and quiet at any time other than bedtime.

The Teulon Treat - This one is super funny, rather unbelievable and a complete embarrassment to The Kidlings so The Hub says I can't write about it! If you see me in person, you can ask me though; he didn't say I couldn't talk about it. ;)

Fifty Thank You Notes - I bought fifty cards, fifty stamps, listed the numbers one through fifty on a page and began filling in names of people to whom I wanted to write a card. I Kaizened it down to doing five at a time so that it wasn't too overwhelming. It felt good to do it and I think people really appreciated it.

The Cutting Edge? - My dietician colleague had an unusual challenge for me. When I asked her for a challenge I had correctly assumed it would be food related but wrongly assumed it would be health related. Andrea challenged me to get a sexy Japanese knife and take a knife skills class. As luck would have it, I had already acquired the perfect knife while on holidays in the Bahamas. The Hub and I watched a young entrepreneur expertly chop up our conch salad with this humongous knife. I asked him where he got it and he pointed us to a... get this... a gas station down the road. Ten minutes and thirty bucks later I was the proud owner of a weapon of mass vegetable destruction. I just didn't know how to do any destruction yet. A few months later I met Audra, a hospital cook, and don't even ask me how it happened, but we ended up engaged in a conversation that had to do with knives. She was so excited because she had been taking a knife skills course and, in fact, she had her knives in the trunk of her car. Before you could say chop chop, we were in the kitchen of this small rural hospital having a full-on knife lesson. An hour later, I was ready... for another lesson. ;)

Axe Throwing - We made it a family affair and what I loved about this adventure was none of the eight of us had ever done anything like this before. We were all learning something new at the same time. It was a super fun family night and we were pretty darn good, if I do say so myself.

Books - I gave away fifty copies of my book *When Enlightening Strikes*. Not just to anyone, to someone I thought would actually read it. To someone who wanted it. Not to someone who could hire me but to someone who might benefit from it. I gave one to someone I chatted with in the airport, a person I met on the beach, my CouchSurfing hosts, a sweet flight attendant, a stranger on the plane who was making the gate agents happy, a waitress who paid me a big compliment, a guy who wanted to write a book. Amazing things can happen when you give a little piece of yourself away.

Savasana - I did a 50 Day yoga challenge inspired by my CouchSurfing host and yoga teacher Saturn Roblee. "Do you sit in Savasana after your yoga practice?" Saturn asked me. I knew the correct answer would be yes, but the truth was no. When I finished my ad-libbed, occasional yoga time, I skipped the part at the end when you lie on the floor and just breathe. I had things to do after all. Don't we all? Saturn challenged me to hold Easy Pose (sitting cross-legged with arms behind your back, holding onto your elbows and bent over at the waist) for ten breaths while letting thoughts of gratitude pass through my head. Then to lie in Savasana for a few minutes to let the physical, emotional and spiritual benefits of the yoga I had just practiced, assimilate. Fair enough, I thought I could do that. Then I decided to up the challenge and to add yoga to my everyday routine. Whether five minutes or fifty-five minutes, I would try to do it every day for fifty days and integrate her recommendations as well. It hasn't remained a daily practice but I'm happy to say I do *Yoga with Adriene* on YouTube a couple of times a week. She's good, check her out.

Being Blind - This Try was inspired by legally blind Boston Marathoner Tracy Garbutt and his guide runner Mike Malyk, who had been guests on my radio show. The BB and I set out to see if we could get a glimpse of what it might be like for the two of them. We took a pair of wrap around sunglasses, smeared them with Vaseline, attached ourselves together with a bungee-like rope and set out for a jog. It was—forgive the pun—an eye-opener. As the runner who was visually impaired we both felt trepidation and uncertainty. More surprisingly, we both equally disliked the position of guide, where we felt so much pressure to keep our partner safe. Both of us came away from this experiment extremely grateful for the miracle of sight that we take for granted each day.

Polar Bear Dare - If there are two things to know about me they are; I don't like water and I don't like being cold. So when my BB asked me to do the Polar Bear Dare with her, I was quite sure she was joking. Turned out she was very serious! The cause is good which makes it a wee bit easier. Profits from the Polar Bear Dare go to Kidsport, an organization that helps underserved kids play sports. Marie is difficult to say no to because she comes along with me for most physical adventures I dream up. I don't love her idea, but I love her! Arghgh. This meant I would be plunging into a sawed hole in the ice-covered waters of Lake Winnipeg in February. This will be more brrrrr than I have ever experienced. Did I mention I hate water and cold, especially together! Torture is always more fun with a friend, and apparently also when in costume! So we recruited our friend Pat for assistance and dressed up in white painter onesies and got our faces full-on painted like polar bears. When they blasted our hand-chosen music "Y'all Ready For This" ("Um… no, actually, I'm not") we held hands and jumped in. Well I was kind of pulled in. If it had been up to me I don't think I would ever have left the safety of the ice. The water stung every cell in my body. I'm pretty sure I would have trampled over my first born to get out of that frigid water. The good news was, unlike a marathon where the torture goes on for hours, this torture lasted only a minute and was relieved as quickly as you could get your butt into the nearby hot tub. Apologies to the Mayor on whose lap I accidentally landed. Oops!

Give Anonymously - According to the 13th century Jewish philosopher Maimonides, one of the highest levels of giving is giving anonymously. Well, I can't tell you what happened here or it wouldn't be anonymous would it? Suffice it to say it's a really cool story. I invite you to keep a bill (a big one if you can swing it) folded up in your wallet for an occasion when you just can't not give it away! I hope you try this many times!

Crazy Aunt Jen - I was challenged to take on a new persona. I didn't actually think this Try would happen, but some things have a life of their own. On a girls' trip to Florida with my youngest daughter and my favourite daughter-in-law, we concocted a story one night en route to a lounge. Apparently Ally Becker, a news anchor from Toronto and her sister Sarah Becker, who ran a dog shelter, were in Florida to visit their aunt (me) who was a singer on a cruise ship. We laughed all the way to the lounge perfecting our stories we never imagined we would use. I swear we weren't in that place five minutes when some middle-aged man tried to pick up my twenty-something daughter. Those girls launched into this ruse with so much conviction I practically believed them. So if you are wondering why you can't find me on Snapchat, it's because my name is Crazy Aunt Jen.

Touring a What? - I took a backstage tour of a funeral home. Well, it was less backstage and more underground, as in down in the bowels and behind the false wall (actually) type of tour. I'm trying to guess at this point if you are asking yourself, "How does she find herself in these situations?" Or "Why does she find herself in these situations?" The why is still the first cornerstone of *The Try Angle*–curiosity, wonder, and knowledge. The how is I was chatting with Susan, a client from a hospital in Indiana.

It turns out that Susan's hubby Pat owns a funeral home passed down to him from his dad. Well, we got to talking and I got curious. He

Susan's mom Sharon has the most incredible Bed & Breakfast in Decatur and she makes the most scrumptious fudge (She even lets you scrape the leftovers from the edge of the pot, mmmm, mmmm, good!).

said, "Sure, come on down, come behind this false wall and see all that we do, including embalming." An hour later I had a whole new respect for funeral directors. They have to be part business person, part social worker and part scientist–such an eclectic blend of talents. This experience also validated my decision to be cremated.

Tennis Anyone? - I joined a group of senior women for a Try at tennis. These gals were at least 20 years older than me with rockin' awesome, fit bods. Let's just say that the woman in charge touched my arm part way through the set, tilted her head and said, "Maybe you should take a few lessons dear." Yeah, maybe.

Maybe Stick to Skiing - Speaking of taking a lesson... I can ski down the blue runs with a modicum of success. I mean I don't look terribly out of place. But who are these kids whizzing past me on skateboards without wheels? Sign me up for a snowboarding lesson, although this seems like a bad idea from the get-go! My barely-old-enough-to-shave instructor shows more patience than one should have at his age and spends an hour teaching my BB and I the basics before he leaves us to fend for ourselves. I have no memories of getting down the mountain (okay, hill, it was really more of a hill–but it seemed mountainous to me at the time). What I do remember is sitting on my butt, all bundled up in snow gear and stuck to a board, wondering how the heck I was going to get down the hill in the dark with snow whirling all around me. The next thing I remember is being at the bottom of the hill, er... the mountain, all sprawled out on my back, unable to get up or detach myself from the unfriendly board and wondering how I was going to get to the lift. I did the only thing I could think of at the time, I rolled to it with the board attached to me. I was killing myself laughing as I rolled, imagining how funny I must look to others. I would bet money the lift operator was Snapchatting my lunacy to the delight of his followers!

Duct Tape Designs - More talking with random strangers led to an evening with Duct Tape artist, Todd Scott. That isn't a typo—there are indeed Duct Tape artists and you gotta see some of his most amazingly unbelievable creations. The Hub and I learned how to create a wonderful bouquet of flowers with just tape and an X-Acto knife. We won't be putting the florist out of business any time soon, but it was an interesting (and sticky) evening!

The Boudoir Shoot - Never would I ever have imagined spending the afternoon in a boudoir studio but it happened after Teri Hofford planted this challenge in my head. It scared the bejeebees out of me and that's how I knew I had to do it. Teri has a special gift for empowering women and a very creative way of making it happen. From pre-photoshoot, where she sends you videos of stretches that will get you ready for the shoot, to studio day, where she arranges it all–hair, make-up and a professional sitting in which she leads you with dance-like precision through the moves necessary to pull this off. Even the post-shoot, the viewing, is a classy experience. I was amazed and even proud (not proud enough to show people proud, but you know, a different kind of proud). Let's just say that the biggest benefactor of this was The Hub. He came for the viewing and had no idea what he was about to view. Surprise honey! So yes, I would recommend this unique experience at least once in your lifetime; it's a completely different way to see your body. And guess what?… men can try it too!

Skiing on Water - My friend Nancy challenged me to try water skiing, which is funny because she doesn't water ski–but whatever. You may remember I dislike cold, I dislike water and especially dislike cold water. Add to that the fact I can barely swim. I have to plug my nose or I think I'll die. Non-water skiing Nancy was kind enough to enlist the help of Diane, the resident expert on her lake, to be my teacher. We drove for two hours on the chosen water ski day. I was already exhausted from work travel but you know what it's like to try to coordinate a bunch of busy people's calendars, it was really our only choice. So the fact it was pretty much the only cold day of the summer, overcast, rainy and cool (which explained why no one else was out on the lake) couldn't be cause to change our plans. Armed with a second-hand wetsuit Dianne and her most patient husband (who manned the boat) were the picture of patience while I sat in the boat telling myself that I wasn't too old to be learning this. Sensing my trepidation, fear and nervousness Nancy said, "You don't have to do this you know." "Yes I do. Just because I'm tired, cold, and scared is no reason not to do it." "It's not?" she said,. "I think it is!" We both laughed. I psyched myself up, plugged my nose, plopped over the edge of the boat and awaited instructions. Those wonderful people stuck with me through flop after flop, nose-full after nose-full, through bleeding hands, until finally–weeeee... I was up! It was a feeling of success, freedom, excitement, awesomeness and exhilaration and I never wanted to let go. I think they were just about as happy as I was. I finally let go of the rope and a head full of misconceptions. I love waterskiing–who knew! Maybe Nancy?

The Igloo Try - On what just so happened to be one of the coldest nights of the year, somewhere around -40°C, a group of us slept outside in an igloo barely big enough to house our bodies. On a bed of buckskins, like spoons (literally) nested together in a drawer, I spent the entire night with five other women I had just met. Jill, the igloo builder, explained to us what to do if we had to go pee. We were to kick open the door with our feet but, she warned, if we broke that seal (which she would create from the outside of the igloo by putting a giant snowball in front of the opening to mimic a door) we would never be able to properly close it again from inside the igloo, so we would likely be quite cold. Instead she advised us that it would be best to just squat in the corner inside and pee there. Ummm, no. Let's just say it was a long night. I think I'll stick with the tipi. In summer.

Unicycling - Do you know anyone who owns a unicycle? I didn't think I did until I mentioned to a colleague that I would like to try riding one and he told me he owned two! He graciously lent them to The Hub and me to try and that's when I discovered that, as long as I have a building to hold on to, I can ride a unicycle! Well maybe ride is not quite the right word. As long as I have a wall to hold on to, I can stay upright on a unicycle. Next!

Clowning Around - Along the same lines as unicycling, I also had the interesting experience of being a clown for a fundraising event. In a borrowed clown costume, an orange wig and with my face disguised by paint, I was very excited to put my rookie juggling skills to work (check out "Juggling in the Airport" in *When Enlightening Strikes*). It was such a different experience socializing and having my picture taken with random kids (the ones who weren't frightened of me), being even sillier than I normally am. I had the most fun interacting with people whom I knew but who didn't recognize me.

Mascotting Around - And speaking of being a clown, I also tried being a mascot thanks to my friend Pat who was working for the Canada Games. She called me up one day and said they needed a mascot and I would be perfect. Pardon my lack of modesty, but I was quite certain that I would be an awesome mascot. Who better to be inside a mascot costume than a motivational speaker? Except that I couldn't talk, it was perfect. The Hub was my "handler" making sure the kids didn't step on my tail and also that I could see them because, if they were right below me, I couldn't even tell. I know you are dying to know what kind of animal I was, and I wish I could tell you, but I have no idea what Niibin actually was. It was described as a "magical creature" and, Kara told me if they were going to make a mascot of me this is exactly what it would look like. The takeaway–always wave to mascots; it can be lonely in there.

Olympic Lifting - Fitness competitor and trainer Hélène proposed this Try: completing a technically-sound Clean & Jerk and a Snatch of thirty-five pounds. I don't have any idea what this even means, but she seems to think it's possible, so off we go for a lesson. The Hub (don't you love how he's all tied up in these challenges now?) and I spent ninety minutes in a training facility fit for Olympic weightlifters. Practicing first with a light-weight dowel while visualizing heavy weights, we worked to perfect the technique before they ever let us have any serious weight. It was a lesson in patience and perfection–neither being strong suits of mine. Although we weren't wearing those odd little, suspender-laden, tight onesies you see the weightlifters wearing on TV, we do eventually get to slam the weights down on the floor like they do and to my delight–they bounce.

Race Car Driver? - I really, really wanted to try to drive a race car. Sometimes I have no idea how to make these Try's materialize but often, after I put them out into the universe, it seems things just start to fall into place. I believe we do not need to know exactly how we are going to do a specific something, we just need to know that we are going to do it. So I found myself at the speedway on race day, behind the scenes all suited up in an official, fire-retardant racing onesie and a good solid helmet–safety first you know. I was extremely excited for my first "race" (again I think of it more as an "experience" than a race) so you can imagine my disappointment when I found out that I was too short—too short (This short person prefers the word *petite*.) to drive the car!! Argh, so close yet so far. This reinforced one of the reasons I don't believe that we "can be or do anything we want–some things are just out of our circle of influence and we must say, "Oh," and let them go or risk the downward spiral of disappointment, sadness and/or negativity. I couldn't drive the car myself but I was allowed to be a passenger and, you know what, nausea aside, it was incredibly fun. I was able to experience a much faster race car experience than if I had been the driver. Sometimes in life you get to be the driver and sometimes you get to be the passenger. One experience is not better than the other, they are just different!

Trying on Religions - I didn't get to as many church services as I wanted to, but exploring new religions was on my 50/50 List. I'm not searching for something else, I'm just regretting not signing up for the World Religions course offered at university (though I suppose it's not too late). Anyway, for a long time I've been curious about different religions. First, I visited a church in the Bahamas where people were speaking in tongues and on their knees crying. Next, I attended a Southern Baptist service in Kentucky where I witnessed the dozens of choir members in their matching robes (just like on TV) getting the congregation singing and shouting, "Amen" in unison. At the end of that service I followed everyone downstairs for fried chicken! Finally, I visited a contemporary Buddhist Temple in Florida where everyone sat cross-legged on the floor for three hours listening to the *bhikkhun* (female monk) teach. Each and every experience was eye-opening. I want to experience more!

The Flash Mob - I participated a flash dance mob in our downtown mall and it was 100% fun! Sign me up for another one!

Bungee Jumping - If you get nauseous on a swing set, maybe bungee jumping isn't the best idea. Did it–won't be doing it again. Ever. Enjoy the video of me screaming!

Slacklining - Have you heard of slacklining? A slackline is like a super-long, seatbelt-looking webbing that you attach between two anchors (typically trees) at various levels off the ground depending on your skill level. You step up on the slackline and try to balance; it's a

very humbling experience because at first it is a struggle just standing on it. Once you build up a little confidence you take a step and work toward walking across it–sort of like a tightrope. The pros even do yoga on it (to see my first try with couch-surfing Tony). The Hub and I optimistically bought one and it's a whole different kind of fun and skill. It's slow and methodical. You have to be patient, patient and more patient. It's a great workout for your quads and core. It's still quite unusual so it's a wonderful way to meet people in the park. Many people wander over to see what's going on and many are open to an invitation to try. Slacklining is a great reminder to slow down, appreciate small wins and take things one step at a time. This activity is a keeper for this chick.

None of Your Business - Of course, there are a few Try's for which you will just have to let your imagination run wild. I'm not talking. ;)

Try 29

behind the drums

ONE OF MY FAVOURITE THINGS to do is to get a glimpse inside someone else's world. Well, not in a creepy, peer through your window sort of way, but rather in a way that helps me to learn, grow and appreciate.

And that is the incentive to spend an afternoon with Crash Test Dummies' drummer extraordinaire, Mitch Dorge, for a try at his craft. A south end Winnipeg boy, this guy's heart is as big as his talent. And his patience, as I found out, is even bigger! Did you know when he's not in his studio adding music to our world, he is out speaking to and inspiring students across the country? Yep, it's true. I bet you didn't know that Mitch is also the world's best hugger? Also true.

But I digress…

I am privileged to find myself in Mitch's recording studio for my first, and quite likely my only, drum lesson. To get an idea what this experience is like, imagine an Olympic athlete trying to teach a kindergartener their sport. To say Mitch has to dumb it down is an understatement. This normally fairly competent woman who makes a living multi-tasking is reduced to a puddle of incompetence trying to count and move my limbs in different configurations at the same time.

One and two and three and four, one e & ah, two e & ah, single stroke, double stroke, paradiddles (gotta love that word!) not to mention the twenty-six essential rudiments. Oh man, those Olympic athletes (and Olympic musicians) make things look so easy, but behind the drum set, believe me, it's anything but.

It was a fantastic reminder of how beneficial it is to move away from what we know every so often. To get away from what comes easily and effortlessly to us and be a beginner again. To be terrible at something now and then. To relearn how to learn, how to accept direction, and how to ask for clarification.

Mitch's unending patience, ongoing encouragement and endless talent will never be forgotten. The importance of learning the space between the beats, allowing your whole body to enter the music and having your mind contribute rather than hinder the process, was something I did not expect to uncover.

This afternoon's drum lesson proves, without a doubt, to be one of my hardest Try's. I am overwhelmed with information. I am stressed trying to remember the combos and I am embarrassed that I can't do what is being asked of me. It is quite possibly the longest three hours of my year!

But all was not for not–is it ever? I hear the drums differently in songs now. I will never look at drums, or drummers, the same way again. Mitch sent me home with a shiny new set of drumsticks and directions to practice my paradiddles on a pillow and come back for another lesson. Gasp. Umm, I don't think so, buddy. I bow to your talent and admire your patience, but I think I can safely say this was my first and last drum lesson. I will leave the drumming to the pros.

Onward to another Try.

Try 30

the grand finale

I<small>T WAS</small> supposed to be my grand finale, the final Try in my 50/50 Challenge, the biggest physical challenge ever for me–to run a full marathon. I didn't know then *The Try Angle* would become a way of life for me and the 50/50 List would grow much longer. I had done a couple of half marathons in the past and while I loved the excitement of the day, the cheering of the crowds and the feeling upon completion, I didn't like the training at all. In fact, while many people "love running"–I'd say I tolerate it at best. For years I'd wanted to *want* to run a marathon, waiting for the feeling to appear, but it never did come. So I decided to push it. What if I just declared I was going to run a full marathon and work backwards from there to make it happen?

It just so happened that the Las Vegas Rock 'n Roll Marathon would be happening on November thirteenth, my fifty-first birthday exactly; you can't get a more perfect fit than that. My friends, Michelle from Calgary and Lea from Philadelphia, signed up to run the half marathon that was going on concurrently (How fitting that Lea, who gave me my first challenge, to sing in public, would be there for my last official challenge.), and all three of us had written our first book together a few years back so we knew we could virtually train together and encourage each other to boot! This would make the "close The Strip marathon" in Vegas weekend a sweet little girls' trip! Win-win-win!

Except for the tiny detail that I still dislike running. I think it's my body shape. These hips were designed for birthing babies, not for running. Then again, I'm past that stage now, so I guess I might as well use them for running. All that aside though, I am such a pokey runner that even the race-walkers get ahead of me. This particular marathon, as I found out after I signed up, has a five-hour time limit. In case you are not in the know about marathon times, this is much shorter than the typical time limit of eight hours. Oh well, I'm in it to try, so let the training begin. The months and months and months and months of training. The hour after tedious hour of training. The hurting, crying, complaining, slow-progressing training. In multiple provinces and many states, wherever I am, in the heat, in the rain, training day after day after day. It's funny how it doesn't bother me to miss a workout here and there but I cannot let myself miss a training day. I think maybe I will grow to like it. I think maybe I will find the runner's high. Nada.

It isn't all terrible though; some cool things happen. Like when The Hub decides to keep me company and starts running with me. That's when I find the runner's high–he had it all along! And like Forrest Gump he just keeps running and running and running, and the next thing I know our girls' trip includes him–he went from couch potato to running his first full marathon. What the heck? No, I was happy for him, really.

As marathon day approaches, it is clear I am nowhere near the five-hour finishing mark. The farthest I have run in my training is nineteen and a half miles (approximately) and that took me approximately four hours and fifty-two minutes. That run took me clear across my city and back again and I have to say it was the best run of my life. I was actually happy during that run, though I can't explain why. Maybe I was high?! Umm, runner's high, that is. Still it is not anywhere near good enough to have me off the Vegas strip in time for them to reopen it.

Here's what I know for sure: I am running as fast as I can as far as I can for as long as I can–and if that means five hours, so be it.

On registration day I seek out some information. I head over to the registration booth and let the volunteer know that it is highly unlikely that I will be able to finish in five hours and I ask what the protocol is if I don't reach the finish line within the time limit. The woman behind the counter has "good news" for me. She says, "There is a van that comes around and picks up the people who will not be able to finish, so you actually still cross the finish line." In a van. She thinks this is great news and tells me that I will still get my medal. But to me this is terrible news and I tell her I am not crossing the finish line in a van. I ask what my other options are. She tells me there are no other options–and I literally start to cry. I did not train for months and months to cross a #*@%ing finish line in a van. Double boo. And a hoo. I guess the lady feels sorry for me at this point so she tells me she can move me up to a different "corral". It's kind of complicated (and boring to read about) but essentially what this means is that I will cross the start line earlier which will give me more time to run–good news!

The Vegas Marathon is run in the evening so runners can see The Strip in all its glory. Race day is perfect; we sit around the pool and psyche ourselves up. But with about 40,000 participants in the various levels of the race (3,000 doing the full) Vegas is nuttier than its normal nuttiness and it turns out we misjudged things a tad.

Couple that with our late start (How can we be ready for things that start at four thirty a.m. but not be ready for things that start at four thirty p.m.?) and the fact that someone, not sayin' any names here, decides he has to go wait in the humongous line for the port-a-potty at the last minute, and, well, we miss our corral grouping. We get a late start which means no extra time to run. Boo.

Still it's a beautiful run. As the sun goes down, Vegas lights up and the moon shines majestically. "I'm just going to enjoy this experience," I think. With faux Elvis singing on this corner, faux Cher on that one, and the crowds cheering, it's easy to get caught up in the excitement on The Strip. Plus, I have some awesome friends who are phoning me en route to encourage me. How cool is that?

But after awhile I'm kind of in nowhere-land. The crowd is no longer around and the runners are really spread out and somehow–don't ask me how–I miss a turn. I was just at Mile 12 and now I'm at

Mile 22, what the heck? Only *I* could get lost in a friggin' marathon. Why do I have to turn everything into a story? Why can't I do something nice and regular like other people do? I am so mad and upset. I had trained so hard for this and I swear I'm not ever doing this marathon thing again. No way! This is my once in a lifetime marathon. But I don't know how to proceed from here. "What should I do? Which way should I run?" I'm crying and the fast runners (who really ran to Mile 22) are whizzing by me on target to be finishing soon. They must be wondering what the heck this pokey, crying chick is doing here.

Just then my phone rings. It's my high school friend–turned Uncle (again, long story) Joey. He has been tracking my race. OMG– are people going to think I'm cheating?! I'm all choked up but I explain to Joey what happened. We figure The Hub should be coming along soon and this makes me feel a bit better; maybe the reason this happened is so that we can cross the finish line together. Boy, will he be surprised to see me here!

So with a new mindset, I continue my pace from Mile 22 towards the finish line waiting for The Hub to pass. But he doesn't pass, instead I find myself on the miracle mile where the crowd is cheering wonderfully. They have their arms up to high-five the racers. I feel like a charlatan but I hate to leave them hanging so I high-five everyone while keeping my eyes glued on the road. I get to the finish line and make a decision, I am not crossing it. My five hours are not up and I'm not done with this race. I am running until my five hours are up or they pull me from the course or I collapse, whichever comes first.

I turn around and begin running the course in reverse. Eyes down. I know this is not normal and I can't even imagine what people are thinking. I know what I'm doing but I'm sure not making eye contact while I do it. I run for a couple of miles and hope to see The Hub running towards me at some point, but he is nowhere in sight so I turn around and run back towards the finish line, and miracle mile… again. I wonder if the people high-fiving recognize me; either way I high-five them, eyes glancing up just a wee bit. I arrive at the finish line again and look at my watch. "Dammit, my time is not up, the race is not over, I have to turn around and run the wrong way… again."

I run a few more miles, still don't see The Hub and, in fact, I hardly see any runners. What I do see though, are lights and they're not Vegas lights, they're vehicle lights. To be specific,they are *van* lights. Yep, *that* van. I try to run by and hope the race marshall, or whoever she is, won't notice me, but it doesn't work. She stops and asks me why I am running in the opposite direction of the course. It's a long story I tell her. She tells me that the course is closing and gives me the choice of getting in the van or running to the finish line. This is not a choice. I turn around and run, for the third and final time, down the miracle mile. There are not many people left–no crowds, no marathoners, just a few kind souls cheering like their lives are depending on it. I begin to wonder what they are going so crazy about? I turn around and look behind me–there is nothing but the van. Oh wow, I realize in a flash that they are cheering for me. Really, really cheering for me because I am last and they think I actually ran the whole marathon and that I am truly finishing. I want to explain to them what I did, that I am not really a marathoner, that I got lost, etc., etc. But I don't. They are excited and I'm so grateful that they are here and that they are cheering when they don't even know me. I bring my eyes up to theirs, I match their smile with my own, I high-five them with as much energy as I can muster and I actually cross the finish line.

At this point they are taking down the finish line, putting things in boxes, and cleaning up the mess. There are no bananas or chocolate milks left for me. No warming blanket. No completion medal. No finisher's jacket. Just one lone man standing with a notepad. With pen in hand, he comes over to me and asks if we can talk. He's a reporter waiting for the person who crossed the finish line last; he wants to see if he can get a story. "Oh buddy, have I got a story for you!" I start to cry as I tell him what I did.

Before I leave the holding area someone hands me a medal and a jacket. I find The Hub–he had run an awesome race fully completed in four hours. I collapse in a heap in his arms as I try to explain what happened. I want to throw the stupid medal and jacket into the sewer… I am just so mad at myself.

He is so proud of me! He says, "Who else would have run back and forth and back and forth? Most everyone else would have given up." He makes me feel like a hero for running the entire five hours, for trying and trying and trying. I so appreciate his generous words, but I still don't want to wear the jacket or the medal. I don't feel that I deserve them.

We find our half-marathon friends in the lounge–they are all showered and pretty and at this moment I hate them all. But they love me anyway and praise me anyway and share my pain with me and it helps a little.

Back in the room, the punishment is not over because "they", whoever "they" are, recommend you take an ice cold bath immediately after the marathon. "Can someone please just shoot me now?"

I am physical and mentally spent and more than a little bit cold. I need time to process everything and bed seems like a very good processing place. Happy Birthday to me.

To try — to attempt an activity with the understanding that it may not be successful.

In the morning, things look better, as they often do. I put on my finisher's jacket and my Rock 'n Roll medal and look at myself in the mirror. They are actually quite nice. I reflect upon what I had done, what I had worked so hard for so long, the wrong turn I took, thinking I was at the finish line and having to go back and work harder again and again. That's when I realize that the "race" I ran is a lot like life. We work hard, we screw up, we try again, we get support from others, we go back and forth, round and round, up and down and eventually, eventually we get somewhere at some time. Sometimes we end up where, when and how we had planned and sometimes we don't. Either way, it's actually all good. It's all gonna be good.

I may not have run the conventional Vegas Marathon but I ran my own unique marathon (which is what we are all doing anyway, isn't it?) and for that I think I deserve the medal and the jacket, thank you very much.

I will wear them with pride.

Try 31

one word

I MEET LUCINDA on a flight. She is writing in a journal. Like on paper. With a pen! I know, right? That's a rarity for sure. I comment and the conversation begins… I learn that she has been keeping a journal since 1960; she has shelves and shelves of them. She goes back and reads them sometimes and the one thing she's noticed over the years is that she hasn't changed that much. Names and places are different but her feelings, her values, her core has remained constant over the decades. We talk for two hours, we tell stories and share secrets and by the end of the flight she asks if I will come and burn her journals when she dies. I'm not entirely sure she's joking.

I tell her that I am a tryologist (I just made that up, but it fits!) and I am collecting challenges. She challenges me to pick a single word to represent each place I visit. One word to set the intention for the day or summarize each day, never repeating the same word. I like it and I give it a try. Here is a small sample…

Embark - the day I met Lucinda, starting on a new challenge.

Progress - a full-day board meeting starts out very, very, very badly but slowly turns around leaving everyone more connected than ever.

'Preciation - an elevator door closes on me but the women inside opens it from the inside. In our five-minute encounter she shares with me her idea to send out pre-thank you cards. To appreciate things before they happen. I love it! I have an interesting guest for my radio show and a new friend in Utah. She ends up so validated from my brief encouragement that she does a TEDx talk and writes book about her awesome idea, giving me much more credit than I deserve. Search Tammy Guffey to hear her talk!

Connecting - Celebrating my daughter's birthday, having all the family gathered around the table, laughing and sharing memories. At the park playing with friends, sharing talents and helping one another, meeting and learning about new people, cuddling with my honey in front of the TV. I love connecting.

Discovery - Uncovering another's hidden talents. Like finding a jewel. We all have many things we are good at, but we all have one gift.

Fortuitous - Happening by a lucky chance. I set this word as an intention for the today. A conversation with an old friend appeared out of the blue and offerings for free experiences came to light. I like that word.

Astound - What astounds you? Is it good or bad?

Flow - A rainy day, water was flowing. Got things done, once I started and got into my flow, time raced by and I felt productive and accomplished.

Satisfaction - A run well done, a cake well baked, laundry done, job secured, connected with friends, visited Mom. Shopped, banked, got hair cut. Had a birthday party for my daughter with a fun candy game.

Breakthrough - In anticipation of a five-hour drive to a job in the Northern U.S. I made an unusual Facebook post: A complimentary offer, "I will be on the road driving solo for five plus hours today–if you would like to talk, have a complimentary coaching call, toss some ideas around, brainstorm and/or gently "pick my brain" I will help you the best I can."

Truth be told, I have a negative emotional reaction to that saying, brain-picking sounds painful! I prefer to ask people if I can "tap into their brilliance"—no one has ever said no to that request!

"Do not leave a message, call back if it's busy. I will not be returning phone calls, just answering them." I couldn't have imagined when I made the offer how many wonderful people I would get to speak with (and hopefully help a little bit). Calls came in from folks in Alberta, Pennsylvania, Illinois, Arizona, New Jersey, Ontario and, of course, a few from good old Winnipeg. I didn't even have time to turn on the radio or play my audio books. This was much better!!

Influence - Presented in North Dakota to a Healthcare team of about sixty people. It was a privilege to have the opportunity to influence people who have the opportunity to influence hundreds of others. Influenced a friend who had sold his guitar fifteen years back to go and buy a new one and rekindle his passion.

Trippin' - Five-hour road trip with Marie, no radio required, just great conversation, giggles and story-telling. Roadside picnic, treats in the car and secrets revealed. Shhhh.

Recovery - Both mentally and physically exhausted, today was a day to recover my body and soul. Through talking it out, crying some, having a relaxing massage and enjoying nourishing food, I was gentle with myself and it helped.

Enough - Enough running, enough food, enough work, enough break, enough TV, enough trying to figure out a problem. Knowing when to say when feels good.

Understanding - Today I want to understand things, both people and situations, better so that I am more knowledgeable, patient and kind.

Full - My head is full, my heart is full, my mind is full and my tummy is full. There is much power in stopping just before full. Except for the heart part, that can continue on to overflowing.

That should give you an idea of how to go about the word of the day challenge. I enjoyed the freedom to choose words that encompassed both setting an intention beforehand or words chosen upon reflection of my day.

Try 32

bee happy

THE THREE OF US meet in a hotel lobby in Minnesota for a pretty standard "what do you do" sort of business meeting to see if there is any synergy between our companies. It isn't until after the gentleman leaves that things get a little more interesting. As we ladies are putting on our coats to leave, I asked Kelly what she does when she isn't working. She tells me she lives on a small farm and that she has just started beekeeping.

Beekeeping? Beekeeping. Beekeeping!

We take off our coats and sit down again. "Tell me everything!" I want to know all about this.

We chat and chat and a few months later, on my next visit to the "Land of 10,000 Lakes", she suits me up in beekeeping garb, gives me a brief lesson, hands me a smoker (it generates smoke to keep the bees calm), and off we go to tend to the bees. The sound is magnificent and though I am a little unsure, I am more excited than scared to get a glimpse inside the world of bees. Kelly, who is still learning apiary science, removes the crates, exposes the bees and like a pro takes care of all their needs while I stand by with the smoker (and the video camera!). This super cool experience helps me understand the many things we can learn from bees:

- Bees actually spend 2/3 of their life doing nothing–so "busy as a bee" is a fallacy

- They live within their means. The only resources they have are themselves.

- They work together to accomplish extraordinary things that they couldn't do alone
- They are opportunists, when the conditions are right they capitalize on them
- They prepare for hard times
- They move through a series of jobs before emerging as food gatherers
- In an emergency they can revert to their former occupation
- They share with others, even other species
- They adapt to their surroundings
- They select high quality, untainted food
- They communicate well with their bodies, visually and with sounds and vibrations
- They do many things in their lifetime but only one at a time
- They thrive on collective decision-making

What I think is most cool about this Try, is that it would have never have happened if our business meeting would have been–well, all business.

It was taking the conversation away from business and getting curious about someone else's life that allowed this experience to happen.

$\mathcal{T}ry\,33$

I hate to be vague

I DO hate to be vague; if you ask me about something I will typically turn it into a big, long, drawn out, colourful story (with even more info filling the margins)–that's what I do, I'm a storyteller of sorts. But this is different, this one is not my story to tell. And it's a really different kind of Try.

It will have to suffice to say that I wronged someone years ago. It wasn't a mistake. It wasn't an accident. It was a wrong. I knew what I was doing and I knew that it would hurt this person.

My challenge now was to pull "it" out of the closet, dust it off and try to make it right. Now it was time to try to make amends. To apologize. To answer any questions that the person I wronged may have. To try to make things right.

This was not about alleviating my guilt; my life was moving forward just fine, thank you. This also wasn't about me being forgiven, in fact I made a conscious effort not to ask for forgiveness. This act was about her and how I could help her get past the hurt I had caused her.

I was very, very fortunate. This could have turned out very badly. It could have unearthed a lot of nasty stuff. It could have left me feeling worse than if I hadn't tried at all.

But it didn't.

She must have been surprised to hear from me; she must have been taken aback. She must have been leery and unsure, these things I am guessing. But what I know for a fact was how she responded. She was so gracious, so understanding. She was so exemplary in her actions, her words, and even her appreciation for my bringing clarity to the situation that she literally left me speech-less.

I learned so much from her classiness during our interaction. There was no drama, no hate, no anger. Just a deep sense of trying to understand and a strong desire to move forward.

I take the lessons she taught me and tuck them away. I hope when I am wronged in the future, I will remember this experience and bring graciousness and classiness and yes, even forgiveness, to that incident as well.

$\mathcal{T}ry\,34$

free hugs

I THOUGHT it would be cool to attempt to break a Guinness World Record. Having no special talents that would logically lead me there, this would be a stretch–but where there's a will there is, as they say, a way!

I needed to decide up front what would be a win for me. I wanted to break a record, of course, but more importantly I wanted to have fun, create a great memory, give others a positive experience, and try my best. Now I just had to figure out which record to attempt to break.

After a little research I discovered that there was actually a hugging record, imagine that! This was exciting news for me because I would not have to submerge myself, lock myself in a small box, or hurt myself in some way. I am truly fond of hugging! I had previously gone on a hugging quest, complete with my *Free Hugs* sign, in the Minneapolis airport of all places. To say it didn't go all that well is an understatement. However, when I tried the same experiment at a hospital in Michigan it turned out to be an incredibly moving experience. This confirmed my feeling that sometimes it's not that the idea is bad, it's just that the circumstances, timing, location, etc., may not be ideal. You can hear me tell the whole story on *The Try Angle* page of my site. It's pretty funny.

Armed (pun intended) with my hugging experience, I decide to tackle the task of blowing out the world record for "Most Hugs in a Minute"–yep, it's a thang! Now, as you may or may not know, breaking a world record is kind of a big deal and Guinness does not make it easy by any means. I know that I can do the hugging part,

but that's not enough. I need a crew–some Try's you can do on your own and some you just can't. This is the latter. Enter organizers extraordinaire–the Toastmaster team, sisters Sharon and Keri! They go through oodles of paperwork and line up timers and counters and whistle blowers. They are Gestapo-like in their instructions on how to pull this thing off.

After months of planning, with hundreds of willing audience members ready, three videographers strategically lined up, two photographers snapping for the book and a partridge in a pear tree for good luck, we are technically ready to meet the challenge. The audience has been briefed and their job is harder than mine I think; they have to be tightly packed in a line with their arms down by their sides (think *March of the Penguins*). There is no time to hug me back, they just have to get in, let me hug them and get the heck out of the way as quickly as possible. Admittedly these will not be top tier, quality hugs. There is no time for pleasantries or thank yous or sinking into each other's arms and feeling the stress go away–we need more than one hug per second!

The event day is here and everyone can feel the buzz and excitement in the room–a crowd of complete strangers uniting to

Is there someone in your life who gives you the best hugs? Mitch (that's his second mention in this book. Mitch–do I get bonus points for that?) and Lois are those people in my life. It's like just seeing them and anticipating the hugs reduces my stress. Their hugs are so real and meaningful and sincere and strong and perfect. Ahhh, you know I feel better just thinking about hugging them! One day I will introduce the two of them for the specific purpose of having them hug each other. You'll have to ask them how it went. If you're lucky enough to have one of those special hugs people around you, stop reading and go hug them and enjoy every second!

achieve one fun goal, all of us being a part of something together that we could never accomplish solo. The music amps up and the horn sounds. The task-oriented team, the willing audience and I do our very best but despite numerous tries we are not able to break the record. We sure had a great time trying though!

> **To try** — to attempt an activity with the
> understanding that it may not be successful.

Looking back at my original goals for this Try–having fun, creating a great memory, giving others a positive experience, trying my best and breaking a record, I can see we reached four out of our five goals– who wouldn't be happy with that?

Free hugs are still available and now that we are not in a rush, I'm happy to say the quality is much better!

Try 35

nice for a living

SOMETHING IS DIFFERENT about me now. I told you about Ruby my ukulele, how I fell in love with music in a whole new way and how I accidentally wrote a song–well there is more to the story.

One day Ruby and I meet renowned children's entertainer Jake Chenier. He asks me to play a tune on Ruby and, because I don't recognize him, I play a wee bit of one of my songs. Yikes, I would never have played in front of a real musician had I known! Jake's "Dinosaur" song, it's so fun!

That's when he breaks the news to me. "You need a better uku-lele," he says in no uncertain terms. I am taken aback. Leave Ruby? Sure she is the littlest, cheapest uke out there, but she is mine. She gave me the gift of music, I feel loyal to her. I just can't.

Then Jake says he will take me shopping for a new one. Shopping with Jake Chenier–well, who would say no to that? He was a hero in my house when the kids were little! Off we go to the music store and that's where I meet Luke. Ahhh, Luke–a handsome devil and a stark contrast to Ruby's fun red colouring. Luke is bigger, more seri-ous and in a class of his own with his wonderful shiny wood grain, a built-in tuner and a jack for a DI cable (whatever that is). When Jake strums him, this talented hands make Luke sound magnificent now I just have to have him! He is a sizeable investment and worth an appropriate case so he won't get damaged. I buy him a hard red case with a plush black crushed-velvet lining to protect his neck. I want to call him Jake, in gratitude, but his name is Luke, Luke the Uke, and even though I feel like I'm cheating on Ruby, even though I don't feel I'm an accomplished enough "musician" to have such a beautiful instrument, he is my new friend. I decide I will try to become worthy of Luke. By the way, Ruby understood and took up residence at my mom's place where she is displayed with pride, and played during each and every visit.

Meanwhile, helping me prove to myself that I am not just a "one hit wonder" Luke and I begin to write songs together. Even though it is just for our own amusement and I play only in the privacy of my studio, I love these songs. One song in particular moves me to tears. I don't want to write it; it is not a "motivational speaker, sing along, cheery type of song". It is really poignant. I try to stop writing it but it pours out all on its own, like a baby who is ready to be born. I have no choice.

People ask about my ukes by name now. It's funny, it never felt silly calling my instruments by name or assigning them a gender, it just seemed so natural. It wasn't until I overheard other people talking about them and referring to them by their appropriate pronouns that I thought, "Ya, maybe a little weird." Ah well, it works for me, so I'm going with it!

This song is special and I believe people *need* to hear it. It's called "Nice for a Living." It's about those of us who give our best all day long at work but when we go home at the end of the day our best is all used up and the people who love us most, matter to us most and care about us most end up getting the worst of us. I really feel that is most of us. I imagine that one day I'll inspire my audiences with this song, but at this point in time that seems too big a stretch, so I stuff that thought away.

But it bubbles up again and I think of Toastmasters. As a long time member, I have been a huge cheerleader for the organization because it really does amazing work to increase communication, leadership and speaking skills. It's a safe place to grow and I have watched many people, who were so scared to speak in public, grow wings. And so I think perhaps it will be a safe place for me to try out my song. Gulp.

As I bring Luke to the front of the room and take him out of his case, I explain to everyone how I'm not a musician but I have something I want to share. As I perch atop the wooden stool, with Luke resting on the music stand, I feel the familiar feelings from my first Try when I sang "Stand by Me." This is even worse. Now, not only am I singing, but I have no backup band, I am playing an instrument and I am singing a song I wrote. I feel so vulnerable and exposed. My leg is quivering uncontrollably, my heart is racing and my mouth is parched.

Despite my comfort being in front of crowds, despite the supportive, smiling, encouraging and familiar group, I am petrified. Petrified!

I give it my best; I have to start over three times. Even though I do not need to look at the music, I can't move my eyes from my music stand. I make eye contact with no one but Luke. It is a bit of a blur but when it is over those sweet people give me a standing ovation and send me notes encouraging me to continue this pursuit.

Instead of feeling proud of what I have done, I feel awful. I feel awful because I wrote, what I am pretty sure is a really important song. When I play it alone in my studio, I play it with great passion and conviction. Today, because of my fear, I couldn't properly share.

I know I have to try this public performance again and again and again even though it scares the heck out of me. I Kaizen it until it doesn't scare me anymore. I have to do it until I can play it the same way for an audience as I do for myself.

The next week I go to Toastmasters early; I sit in the corner facing the wall and play while people are coming in and chatting. It's a wee bit better.

The following week I do the same thing except that I play at the break and as people are leaving. It really helps when people aren't paying attention.

The fourth week I do the same thing, but this time I turn my stool around so I am facing the people, my eyes still staring at my music stand.

At the next meeting, you guessed it–I did the same thing, but this time I stand up and try to make eye contact. I feel a bit more comfortable with each performance.

Since that time I have sung my songs, and especially this particular song, in front of thousands of people all over the country. I am still not a "musician", I am a speaker who sings a message. I have forgotten the words many times, I have played the wrong notes and done many more imperfect things as I "performed". But you know what? It didn't matter, because, as I had hoped, the message of the song overpowered the performance. When this imperfect song causes a standing ovation, it's certainly not because of my musical talent–it is because the words resonate with the audience; it's because the acknowledgment of the Try exceeds the results. Even if I speak the exact words in the song during my program, there is something about the combination of the words *and* music that grips people at their core. I see tears streaming down people's faces. I hear stories of how the song affected these people and what they did differently in their life as a result of hearing it. I believe to the core of my core that this song matters and has the potential to make people better than they were.

If I'd have waited until l was ready to perform it perfectly, if I'd put my big ego ahead of the message, if I'd cared so much what others thought that I couldn't share the music–all those people would have missed out. I would have missed out.

Doing things for the first time can be scary. Doing things you aren't comfortable with can be scary. Doing things you aren't good at is scary. Risk is, well, scary!

But what I know for sure from personal experience is I always, yes always, come out on the other side better than I was before I started. And this Try was no exception.

During a long stopover in New York, I was looking for a private place to kill time and play Luke without disturbing anyone. I settled for a bench in the ladies room, tucked my case under the bench and began to play. I thought that between all the bathroom noises and the short time the ladies are in there, I shouldn't be too much bother. Imagine my surprise when a lady came over to give me a dollar! "I don't know if you want money, dear," she said, "but you sound just lovely!" I was so shocked that when she insisted I take it, I asked her to sign the bill for me. I keep it in Luke's case, proof that I am a paid musician!

Try 36

one small step

WHEN I WAS FIRST collecting suggestions for my 50/50 List many people threw very big ones my way–climb Kilimanjaro, go to Machu Picchu, walk the Camino de Santiago, do the Pacific Coast Trail–they all sounded like devine experiences but, keeping in mind that I still have to work and that I don't have an unlimited budget, it was clear that not everything on the list could be done during that year. But the ideas remained tucked away in my psyche for "maybe someday".

Surprisingly someday came quite sooner than I thought it would when my friend Ruth Bonneville invited me to join her as she rang in her fiftieth birthday with a hike on the Inca Trail which leads to Machu Picchu. Up from my psyche bubbled that challenge I had tucked away. Yes was the only option. I was happy to have my very fit Middle-est join us on this expedition, and with all the enthusiasm we three adventure seekers could muster we set out on this Peruvian exploration.

In retrospect, a little research on my end would have been a great idea. Little did I know that the "hike" was actually the Camino Inca, a twenty-six plus mile, four day trek almost entirely up the ancient Inca-built stone steps. Nothing could have prepared me for this challenge, except perhaps watching the documentaries, reading, researching, training–well, I guess a lot could have prepared me, but the truth was, I didn't prepare.

The first day of this expertly guided hike turns out to be very difficult; quickly our group of twelve disperses as everyone falls into their own pace and leaves me firmly planted in–where else? Last place, unable to see anyone behind me or anyone in front of me.

You'd think I'd be used to this by now, but when I finally come upon the group all sitting together waiting for me so that they can have their lunch, I feel the tears well up. This is just the first morning, how the heck am I going to do this? They had warned us that the second day was the worst, eight hours up stairs of stone, on the edge of mountains. There is no going back. Even if you die, they carry you forward... helicopters can't even get in there. Good grief, why do I get into these messes? Never mind, I guess I know why.

The group we are with is led by Llama Path, who I highly recommend. The guides are all top notch, the porters (built like little fridges and carrying about that amount of weight) are amazing and the food was akin to what you get on a cruise ship—no joke, it is amazing. The porters carry everything we need to camp. They run ahead of us, set everything up, then take it all down after we leave in the morning and run ahead to the next campsite. It's an incredible sight to see. As I am huffing and puffing this little man runs up behind me carrying my hiking boots and pole. I notice that he's wearing sandals and jeans and basically hoisting my weight in supplies on his back. It makes me feel ridiculously bad for complaining.

But... despite feeling ridiculously bad complaining, here it goes anyway... the altitude sickness hits hard, my stomach is not right, my head is not right and despite chewing on the recommended cacao leaves it's a bear to deal with. Plus the cardio is insane; I'm in quasi good shape but my heart has never felt this way–it feels like it's going to leap out of my chest. My breathing is so laboured and I wonder if this is what people with asthma or COPD or even smoke inhalation feel like. Everything hurts and it's not like I can just shuffle along because there are stairs. I must lift up for every step I take, and even going down (I swear there isn't a flat mile within the whole twenty-six miles) I am pounding down each and every step. Additionally, while I'm complaining, I'm petrified throughout the hike for a variety of reasons. Sometimes it's because I can't see anyone else and I think maybe I've gone the wrong way (again). Sometimes it's because the cliffs are so steep with no protection from falling, and sometimes it's because I just plain think I'm going to die. Oh yes, I should mention that our little party of three is at another disadvantage–the airline had somehow lost our luggage. All of our equipment and clothing are newly purchased, not worn in or tested or what we had carefully shopped for and broken in in the weeks prior to the trip. Then throw in the rapidly changing weather (for which we are carrying many changes of clothing on our backs)–from sweltering heat, to freezing cold, to pouring rain and even hail. Hail? Seriously do we really need to add hail? When we finally reach our campsite each night we are wet, cold, sore and cranky. Then we get to sleep on the ground... how awesome is that! And we paid for this experience! This is supposed to be *camino*–a pilgrimage, a time to reflect on one's life. How am I supposed to reflect on my life when I'm so busy just trying to stay alive. This was not a camino to me, this was survival.

Okay, I'm done complaining now.

Upon reflection, the Camino Inca was a most incredible experience. I was so blessed to have my friend and most especially my Kara, with whom to share the laughs, tears and wins. It was an unforgettable journey for all of us. I have traveled the world but never have I seen such beautiful natural wonders as I did on this four day trek. I felt so privileged to be in that sacred space to view the same vistas as the Incas had over 600 years ago–the space that can only be experienced by walking the path. Thousands take the train to Machu Picchu, it is busy with tourists like a Peruvian Disneyland of sorts, but so few get to see all the amazing Inca sites along the way that are the reward for making the trek. I am so grateful for my body, despite its ailments, and my mind, despite its ailments, had the capability to get me through day after day of what I believe was the hardest mental and physical challenge I have ever experienced. I appreciated the food (especially the vegetarian cuisine prepared just for me), the talented hands that prepared it, and the strength and grit of the porters who made us as comfortable as possible given the circumstances. I loved our guides' energy, enthusiasm, patience, direction and love for the culture they were sharing. I loved sharing our adventure with a new group of friends from all over the world and all walks of life who supported and cheered each other on.

On the trek, when I stopped for a breather, I thought about my one to ten scale. Ten, charging ahead, leading the pack; one, giving up. I'm not getting anywhere staying in one place. I thought about my four percent. One small step at a time, one step matters, one step is closer to where I need to be. Four percent, sometimes it's a physical reach and sometimes it's a mental one. It's how we can prepare for the next step, psyche ourselves up for the next step, and talk ourselves into actually taking that step…

Lots of people ask me if I'd recommend the Camino Inca. It's not a simple question to answer. It's definitely not for everyone. I'm not even sure it was for me. I really feel like someone else completed this incredible journey; that this body and mind couldn't have. But this body and mind did and nobody seems to care if I came in last, again.

Try 37

¡tu vida, ilimitada!

FOLLOWING the luggage losing fiasco in Peru, we had to repurchase/ replace every little thing for our hiking expedition. Even if you love shopping (which I don't) this was not a fun experience. We were under a severe time restraint and we had to go out of the tourist area to get the specialized things we needed. We found ourselves in a local shopping mall, very North American-like except for the language. Hardly anyone spoke English, making this frantic shop even more difficult.

Following this shopping spree I think it interesting how, even though we were in their country, we were frustrated by the fact that people don't speak English. In retrospect, the three of us, knowing for months we were going to a Spanish speaking country, didn't even bother to study even a few words of their language. Interesting and slightly disturbing to me.

With the help of Google Translate, I was able to make our needs known and communicate, albeit clumsily, with the staff. It wasn't long before Kara and Ruth were asking me to translate or to ask the clerks something, and the clerks were responding to me to tell Kara and Ruth the answers. It was at that moment, like a light switch, that I make a decision.

I've always thought Spanish was a beautiful language and I've always been envious of people with linguistic skills. Other people have those skills, not me. It's not like I thought "someday" I'll learn; I had already written it off. "I'm too old to learn. Too bad I didn't learn as a child. I'm not linguistically gifted. I'm not smart enough…, etc." Those old recordings kept droning on and on.

I make a decision that day in the shopping mall in Peru–I am going to try to learn Spanish. Maybe not perfectly, maybe not fluently, but next year at this time I will have words in my back pocket that I can use to communicate better. I will show respect for the Latin communities I visit by at least attempting to use their native tongue.

And so I am on a mission to figure out how many different ways can I integrate Spanish into my life. I can watch a TV show and program Spanish subtitles. I can learn a Spanish song. I can take a course. I can turn my Facebook language to Spanish. I can enlist the help of a Spanish friend. And… there is, of course, an App for that! I can use Duolingo!

Duolingo, if you haven't heard of it, is a second language learning platform that has both free and a premium level. I'm hooked. It's daily reminder makes it hard to ignore your commitment. Every day, magically, I *find* time to do this. I am spending from five to thirty minutes each day on this App and I am committed to improving my ability to communicate in Spanish. I am having a blast doing everything from learning my *español* ABCs with *Sesame Street*'s Elmo on YouTube to practicing the Spanish love song, "Cielito Lindo" (you know it, it's the Frito Bandito Corn Chips song–ay, ay, ay, ay, but it has real Spanish words–who knew?).

No hablo español perfecto pero hablo mejor que antes! This means, I do not speak Spanish perfectly but I speak it better than before! Besides being really good for your brain, studying a new language forces you to keep a beginner's and a learner's mindset, which is humbling (Why won't my tongue wrap around that Spanish word?!) and adds a healthy respect for those who are multilingual. It also bubbles up a certain pride that comes from actually having actually tried.

Tu Vida, Ilimitada is my business name–*Your Life, Unlimited*–in Spanish, and really, what other way do you want to live life?

Think about something you would like to learn or maybe have always wanted to learn, and imagine all the different ways you can open up your life and let the learning in.

Try 38

give it away

NOT SO MUCH challenged by, but simply inspired by Kirk Stivers, my vegetarian, minimalist, motorcycle riding, CouchSurfing host in Florida, I set out on a quest to give away fifty things a week for five weeks.

Kirk, who was in my life for a mere forty-eight hours, turned out to be one of the most together, happy and content (and unknowingly influential) people I had ever met.

The guy owned less "stuff" than anyone I knew. He was the first real minimalist that I had ever met and when I returned to my suburban bungalow, I now looked at everything inside it with fresh eyes.

I look around at all the stuff we have—on the walls, in the closet, in the garage, in the cupboards–and I ask myself this question, "Do I love this?" I am surprised to find out how few times the answer is yes. Sometimes it is something I need but very rarely is it something I love. What an awakening!

Even though we are not pack rats, things do accumulate after three kids, four pets, and twenty years of living in the same house. Suddenly I'm on a decluttering mission–get out of my way!

Fifty items a week–where to begin? I decide that each week I will go into five different rooms and remove ten items from each room. I admit it was a little bit hard at first (you know how you get attached to stuff!). Sometimes the ten things would mean ten pens–I mean do I really need 276 pens commemorating every hotel I have ever visited? No, I need five pens that work really well.

Do I need this shirt that I haven't worn, these pants that don't fit or this scarf that I don't even like? No, I will keep the clothes that I love, that fit and that I wear.

Do I need this knick-knack because Auntie Fran gave it to me, this pot because it was my mom's or this picture because it's "valuable"? No, I will the keep things I love and/or use.

Do I need to keep every owner's manual (for things that have long since broken and hey, isn't everything online these days now anyway?), every key (I'll never figure out what this one is for), every piece of sporting equipment (Do we even still like that game?), all this jewelry, these board game, kitchen utensil, and half-empty cans of paint? No, no, no.

I don't know if I can adequately explain how wonderful it feels to open up the pots and pans cupboard and be able to get what you want with ease, to look into your closet and see just the clothes you like and wear, or to actually be able to close the file cabinet drawer for a change. It feels so wonderful that just thinking about it makes me smile.

For me the hardest things to get rid of are my books. Hundreds of (mostly) personal development books lined up row after row in a huge bookcase custom made with love by a client. Books that I had used for research, education and enjoyment. Books written by friends, or people that I had interviewed and admired. Signed books, personalized books. Books that made me feel smart, special, and valued. How could I get rid of those?

Each week I slowly pull books off my bookshelves and they compete with each other, seeming to say, "Keep me—give that other one away." They cajole me and whisper reasons why they should be kept. I can hear them… "You'll read me again. You need me for research. I have your name signed inside. You actually like this author–she's your friend!" Argh! Make them stop please.

I try to quiet the noisy books. Each week I give away to specifically chosen friends who I think will appreciate a particular title, but after awhile, once I am really latched onto decluttering, a brilliant idea comes to me. Instead of picking out a few publications I am willing to part with, I will pick out the few that I really want to keep. The rest I mercilessly pack up in boxes, bring to a public event where I announce, "Take with your hands, pay with your heart. All the money collected will be donated to help build a school in the Congo." It was much easier to give them away knowing that others would benefit.

Getting rid of things turns into a bit of an addiction. The Hub and I realize we are on the cusp of a new life. Married at twenty-two and bringing our first born home just one year later, followed by two more kidlets within the next four years, we had spent the great majority of our time together as parents. The wonderful, all-consuming busyness that comes with raising a family lends itself perfectly to collecting stuff in various sizes, colours and types. With the news that our baby, our last little bird, had purchased her first house, we decide

A couple of years ago I had a random conversation with a gent from the Seattle area. Since I had never been there, I asked him what it was like. He would have no idea that what he said next would change my world. He said, "I can't imagine living anywhere else." I was in awe as the words sunk into my head. I suddenly realized that I had never lived anywhere where I could say, "I can't imagine living anywhere else." I didn't know where that perfect place was for me, but I knew I wanted to find it. Pair this revelation with the response of a taxi driver down south who replied with some distaste "Why do you live there?" when I told him where I was from. I told him about the cost of living and the nice people, yadda, yadda, but when I got home to my Winnipeg, the only city I had ever known, it suddenly hit me, "Why do I live here?" It was because my dad was transferred here when I was three years old. That's the reason I live here. Because no one ever told me, and I didn't figure it out for myself, that I could live somewhere that I truly loved. Suddenly the reason didn't seem that great anymore and, for the first time, I realized that I probably don't have to bloom only where I was planted. I could bloom anywhere. We can bloom anywhere!

to make a major shift. It is time to right size. We need a change and the time is right!

So, the same day we find out our daughter has purchased her first home, we put ours up for sale on a free online website with only these few words to describe it–*Thirteen hundred square foot bungalow filled with love.*

Her name is Karleigh and she calls right away requesting to come and see the house. I'm not prepared for that. I tell her that we aren't really ready to show it, there is spring dog poop that has yet to be taken care of.

"That's okay, we'd like to come." So, I tell her that the house hasn't been staged, and not only that, it wasn't even clean!

"That's okay, we'd like to come." Now I tell her about the leak in the master bathroom and that there are holes cut out of the drywall in preparation for having it fixed.

"That's okay, we'd like to come."

So they come the next day with their beautiful six-month-old little baby, Kendell, in tow.

I show them around a bit, but I'm not prepared to open the door of Gina's room because you can't even see the floor for all the clothes scattered about. "If you are interested in the house, we'll get that room cleaned up," I say, "We're interested, please open the door." Argh! With an apology for what they are about to see, I reluctantly open the door.

Right there, right then–no dickering, no haggling, no back and forth–they offer to buy the house for the exact amount we are ask-ing. We sign some papers and are now officially homeless.

We have no idea where we are going to live or what we are going to do. We just know that we aren't going to be living here anymore. Such an odd, melancholy feeling. Excitement for what's to come and sadness for all that will be left behind–the walls that have watched our family grow up, the mural corner fence that wraps our house in love. Now it is time for this house to watch another family grow up. I am happy for them.

Getting rid of things takes on a whole new meaning. Now it is not just a want to, it's a have to. We may not know where we are going but one thing we know for sure is that we aren't taking all this stuff with us.

We look at smaller houses, we look at condos and we check into renting in our city. Then one day I find myself at a speaking job on Vancouver Island, a beautiful place where The Hub and I had vacationed years before. We had loved, loved, loved it here–maybe I should look at properties here. The Hub gives the nod and says that if I see something I love I should go ahead and buy it. He reminds me that if need be we can always rent it out for a couple of years until we are ready to move there. I turn around and click my heels and before I am on my way home I have bought a condo, invited The Hub to quit his job and made a plan to move to the island in four months. I don't know how it happened, but it did. It was magical.

Many have asked and many more have wondered so I will answer... "How could you leave your kids?" Well, we are fortunate enough to have three capable, competent and contributing members of society. They each have stable careers in the helping professions and they all have significant others who love them and whom we love. Of course we will miss them, but the country is small and if any of them call at breakfast, we can be there by lunchtime. The kids have their own lives and we will visit often–that's how. Plus I have 'Something About Mary's' circle in my head. It's our time! The harder thing for me was leaving my mom. Maybe that isn't a squirrel, I think it's a whole new chapter.

Try 39

live your life

I TRY to visit my mom every day when I'm not on the road speaking. She lives happily in an assisted living residence and always says, "It's like every day is a vacation."

Often when I come, I bring Luke the Uke and play her favourite songs. Sometimes we play crib, sometimes I bring my dog Cosmo or a friend of mine to add a little spark to our visit. Sometimes she is napping in her bed and I curl myself around her and cuddle. It's been over twenty-seven years since my Dad died, since she has had someone beside her to cuddle–she loves it when I do that.

And so it was, months before we sold the house, I found her in her toasty bed in the middle of a wintery Sunday afternoon and I crawled right in. I wasn't planning to ask, but as we lay together with my face to the back of her head, I felt safe. The question that had been on my mind for some time just bubbled out.

"How would you feel if we moved away?" I asked tentatively. She didn't even skip a beat. In an unwavering tone she said, "You need to do what makes you happy. You need to go where you want to go. I've had my life. I will miss you terribly but I know you love me and I know I will see you again, so I think if you want to go you should go, and you shouldn't let me or anyone else stop you."

As she speaks, I feel the tears streaming down my face. It's not that her answer surprises me, I was quite sure that the essence of what she would say would be, "Go," but hearing her voice, tone and certainty took my breath away. Even after spending her entire life giving to her four kids, at a time when she deserves to be selfish (she is in her nineties, after all) and could easily play the needy card, she continues to give wings to the ones she loves, and she gives it with conviction.

This woman, without fanfare, continues to inspire me and others, proving that you don't need to get on a stage, make a social media post or, as in this case, even leave your bed, to make a lasting impression on someone. I hope I can continue to give gifts like this to my children.

Last stop, my sister. If I move, I will be the third sibling to leave the province and this will mean she will be the sole caretaker for our mom. She too gives me her sincere blessing. And so, it seems we are moving four provinces to the west. With us we are taking only what will fit into a small five by eight trailer–and I can tell you that won't be much. Along with the house, we sell my sweet little convertible so that we can purchase a very practical (and much less fun) truck. We will be a one vehicle family for the first time ever! And while this is a little more than I had planned with the "Give it Away" Try, we give away almost everything we own. In retrospect, I wish we would have given all of it away. We should have just packed a couple of suitcases and started completely fresh.

We have a modest condo, just over a thousand square feet, on

Vancouver Island. The town is called Sidney, Sidney by the Sea. It's about thirty minutes north of Victoria, the capital of British Columbia. The condo has sixteen foot ceilings, big tall windows and hardly any furniture. We have a massage table where a dining room table should be and the one extra room serves as the guest room, office, yoga studio and music room. Thank goodness for Murphy beds!

The changes we have made in a very short time have been plentiful, among them–house to condo, big city to small town, two vehicles to one vehicle, nesters to empty nesters, pets to no pets, two jobs to one job, prairie to coast, and a huge community friends to barely a few. It has been an emotional roller coaster, but what I know for sure is that I love where we live. Every day, multiple times I say out loud, "I love it here!" Here in our condo, here in our block, here in our town. Every day I see the ocean and it fills me up. Every time I hear the horn blow from the ferry, I smile. When I'm flying to my new home and I see the mountains, hills, water and flora I say a silent thank you to all who made it possible for me to be here–my kids, my mom, my sister and of course, The Hub.

Each day we run, hike, walk and enjoy the outdoors like we never have before. People ask us, "Why here?" to which I always answer in one word, "Lifestyle." I love living where I can enjoy the lifestyle. I love that I can enjoy it numerous times every day, not just on weekends or holidays.

Our new town has a population of under 12,000–quite a far cry from the 750,000 that we left. This wee town has beautiful little shops and a bakery that opens its doors first thing in the morning and fills the whole street with the best smells. In this sleepy little town you could run down the main street naked after 6 p.m. and no one would take notice. The Walk Score, which measures the walkability of your particular area, is high. The bike paths are second to none, and hiking, blackberry picking and kayaking are minutes away. When bigger-city needs beckon we can be in Victoria, BC's capital, in under thirty minutes and find all the amenities we need and more. Did I mention I love it here? I do. Of course, change is hard and there are many things to miss about our "old" world, but never in my life have I wakened every morning and said, "I love living here." And I like that!

I saw a magazine called *Beautiful British Columbia* at a friends house, it was an old magazine from 1975 and when I saw it I all but wept. A flood on memories came back to me. I was a little girl, sitting on the floor leafing through this magazine. They were delivered to our house monthly because my dad was a fruit buyer for grocery stores. Every month I devoured these magazines wondering where this gorgeous place way. I knew when I saw that old magazine at her house my soul has been here since I was a child. It just took this long for my body to catch up.

#grateful

Part Three

the next new beginning

future
challenges

FUTURE CHALLENGES, in case they spur a thought in your head you'd like to try:

Three in One - Since the Camino Inca didn't end up being the soul-searching camino I had envisioned, I will explore doing at least some of Camino de Santiago in Spain where hopefully some of my newly minted Spanish will be helpful. And maybe, since my challenge of living a month in a different place turned into moving to a different place, I'll consider staying in Spain for a month. And while I'm there, I may as well run with the bulls. Kidding, totally kidding! Never, no way, nada, poor bulls, PETA (People for the Ethical Treatment of Animals) and I would never support that.

Open Doors - The Grateful CEO, Steve Foran wants me to mimic his experiment and go to a local mall, coffee shop or office building (or any combination thereof) and open the door 100 times for other people.

Makeup - Inspired by my non-makeup wearing friend Kate McKenzie, who challenged herself to wear makeup every day for thirty days, I want to go without makeup for thirty days and also wear makeup everyday for thirty days. I think both will be a challenge for me.

Go Vegans! - I think I'm willing and just about ready to try veganism for 30 days.

Compliment a Stranger - I think I am pretty good at giving random compliments but I would like to be purposeful and intentional about doing this very day for thirty days too. Dr. Larry Ohlhauser has attempted to compliment someone he does not know every day for over twenty-five years. Every day! He says he has stories that would fill a book and this simple act constantly reminds him to be grateful. Love it; let's all do this one!

Someone Else's Shoes - I would like to "break" my arm or leg, bind a hand, wear noise cancelling headphones and wear a blindfold (not all together) for a full day to get a sense of what it is like to have each of these challenges. This might help me understand how others experience life and appreciate what we able-bodied people take for granted.

Bouncing - A trampoline class sounds fun, but I feel like after three kids it might not be the best idea. ;)

Signing - I would like to try to learn a song in American Sign Language. It looks so beautiful and would help me appreciate and communicate better. Maybe "O Canada" would be appropriate!

Play in a Band - Maybe my microphone would be turned off and my instrument would be unplugged, but I'd like to try practicing and playing even just one song with a group.

Co-write - Staying with the music theme, I would like to co-write a song with someone.

No Complaining - Friends since we were teenagers, Dr. Dean Schrader challenged me to go for twenty days without complaining. I'm a pretty positive person but even I think this is going to be hard. I challenged him to do this with me. I'm ready when you are Dean!

Naked Wonder - My BB, Marie... remember her? She may be crazier than I am! She challenged me to go twenty-four hours naked. This will require some serious planning (and blind drawing). I may negotiate to going twenty-four hours in undees; I'm not as crazy about going braless as she is. ;)

Playwright - I would like the challenge of writing a play.

Spartan Racing - My daughter Kara is into Spartan Racing and I would like to join her for an event, even if it's just to be in her dust and/or her cheerleader.

House/Pet Sitting - The Hub and I are exploring some house/pet sitting sites to see how we can make exploring our world feasible while at the same time enjoying some four-legged friendships. If you know someone who is looking, give them our card!

Love Everywhere - I was sharing some amazing stories from my *Love Everywhere* project (365 days of sharing beauty, love and kindness with the world) and my colleague Paul Huschilt said, "You *must* write that book." That's coming up!

Lies? - An audience member challenged me to not tell the truth for 24 hours. Honestly, I don't think I can do this one. Then again, maybe I'm lying. ;)

Spelunking - I mean who wouldn't want to do this, just based on the coolness of its name. Also called caving or potholing, it's the recreational pastime of exploring cave systems. Sign me up!

Bouldering - Along the same lines as spelunking, I'd like to try the rock climbing-like sport of bouldering.

Aboriginal Experience - I would like to be educated about and experience a sweat lodge, a pow wow or some sort of Aboriginal ceremony.

Fasting - I'm psyching myself up to do a twenty-four hour fast. So far I haven't managed to get past seventeen–I'm slowly working my way up.

Photojournalism Plus - My friend Ruth is a photojournalist. I would love to spend a day working with and learning from her. In fact, I would spend a day at just about anyone's workplace to see things from a different angle. I asked if I could work at Starbucks but they said no. Boo.

I wrote an awesome mini-book for Starbucks, which I sent to their head office for review. The sent me a cease and desist letter. That was so sad–in my mind it was a really clever idea!

Sleeping - Not just regular, in-my-comfy-bed type of sleeping. Did you know you can sleep in a tree, a tree! And also under the stars in mountain pods? Ahhhh, those are on my list.

Stand-up - I'm shuddering as I write this lest I actually have to try it, but I know that trying stand-up comedy would help my speaking career, give me an even greater respect for those in comedy and push me out of my safe space for sure.

Record a Music Video - I am going to try to have *Nice for a Living* professionally recorded and a music video made so that more people are able to experience its message. I have no idea how I'm going to do this, but I'm putting it out there!

This and Tat - No, that wasn't a typo! When I was first telling people about the 50/50 List a number of them suggested 50 would be a great year to get a tattoo. Wow, a tattoo, that was certainly a permanent marker of turning 50. I was sort of waiting for the invention of the five-year tat, that might be something I could commit too. I wasn't sure what I could commit to for life. I was on the fence with tattoos in general, neither opposed nor excited. I remained open-minded but not committed. What I did know was that, if I ever did get one, it wouldn't be just for the sake of getting one, it would be meaningful, special and a perfect fit. But then, a trip with my daughter Gina changed everything. She suggested that the three of us, (me, her and her sister) all get matching tats. Instantly I knew I could commit to that for life. I didn't even care what the tat looked like, just the thought of all of us having the same one affected me to my core. And then the idea got even better. We would get a lily, in honour of my mom Liliana, who has been a constant source of support, love and laughter to our family and who still keeps us on our toes. A beautiful tribute to my past—my mom, and my future–my girls. A constant reminder of such important gifts. Perfect. I told my sister and my niece about the idea and I think that they are in too. Most surprisingly, when I told my mom, she said she would get one as well. What?? How cool is that! Now, if we can just agree on the appropriate lily, we will be good to go. Stay tuned.

Your Turn - If you have a challenge for me or something you would like me to try, send it my way–I promise to give it fair consideration and hey, maybe we can even do the Try together?!

never
be
the
same

In **2015**, when I was turning 50, if someone would have told me that in less than two years I would be a short-haired blond, vegetarian, songwriting, ukulele playing, minimalist who had climbed the Andes and was now living on a west coast island, I would have doubled over in laughter.

But that's what I am. *The Try Angle* worked for me and I know it can work for you.

As you have read numerous times now...

> **To try** — to attempt an activity with the understanding that it may not be successful.

My greatest desire in writing this book was that I would be able to convince you that the rewards of trying and the benefits of change are worth so much more than the risks. I truly hope you will put *The Try Angle* to work in your personal and professional world so that you can enjoy a new slant on your already blessed life.

I would love to know what Try you are going to pursue as a result of reading *The Try Angle* and, of course, I would love to hear the results of your attempt! Maybe I will compile reader's stories for *The Try Angle Too!*

As for me, I've gotta go. I've got a boatload of things to try and only a couple of decades left to squeeze them all in!

P.S. Thanks for picking up my book and for reading right to the end. Unless of course you skipped to the end. Did you? If you did, go back–you missed some really funny stuff! I had a great time writing this for you and reliving these experiences. I highly recommend you write down your Try's too–it's like having the fun all over again!

Please visit Steph's website
YourLifeUnlimited.ca/Try

to see videos and pictures of some of her Try's
and some items of interest that she referenced.

Why am I talking in the third person all of a sudden?

If your organization, team or group would benefit from ideas, insight and inspiration I'd love to talk to you about creating a win-win! YourLifeUnlimited.ca/contact.

To these folks, and more, who knowingly or unknowingly, inspired, helped, pushed, pulled and/or dragged me (and others) to the next level:

Mary Alberding, Lorraine Baydack, Kassy Bouchard, Lois Braun, Lea Brovedani, Lana Bullough, Gina Carr, Michelle Cederberg, Jake Chenier, Mitch Dorge, Pegine Echevarria, Tony Esteves, John Foilet, Audra Fravel, Barry Friedman, Tracy Garbutt, Marie Gledhill, Sharon Golin, Tammy Guffey, Nancy Heinrichs, Rainer Hersch, Teri Hofford, Tim Hurson, Karen Jacobson, Jen Joyal, Lucinda Kelly-Smith, Martin LaTulippe, Kerri Lipischak, Mike Malyk, Hélène Massicotte, Gentil Mis, Barbara Neray, Sierra Noble, Dr. Jill Oakes, Dr. Larry Ohlhauser, Jessica Pettitt, Kelly Prchel, Dr. Dean Schrader, Todd Scott, Susan & Pat Sefton, Lori Smith, Aaron Staples, Gina Staples, Kara Staples, Randy Staples, Joey Ste. Marie, Kirk Stivers, Tracy & Maurice Thibodeau, Tracy Tjayden, Sharon Walters and Cheryl-Ann Webster.

If I missed you, forgive me, I really tried!

Made in the USA
Middletown, DE
03 May 2021